Also By Marjorie Doyle

Books

Reels, Rock and Rosaries:
Confessions of a Newfoundland Musician

Newfoundlander in Exile:
The Life and Times of Philip Tocque (1814-1899)

A View of Her Own

Film

Regarding Our Father
(co-written/directed with John W. Doyle)

A DOYLE READER

Writings from Home and Away

MARJORIE DOYLE

Introduction by Shelagh Rogers

BOULDER
PUBLICATIONS

Library and Archives Canada Cataloguing in Publication

Doyle, Marjorie M.
    A Doyle reader : writings from home and away / Marjorie
Doyle.

A collection of personal commentaries and columns.
Issued also in electronic format.
ISBN 978-1-927099-15-5

    1. Doyle, Marjorie M. I. Title.

PS8557.O928D69 2013   C818'.5409   C2013-900347-9

Published by Boulder Publications
Portugal Cove-St. Philip's, Newfoundland and Labrador
www.boulderpublications.ca

Copy editor: Iona Bulgin
Design and layout: John Andrews

Printed in Canada

Newfoundland
Labrador
We acknowledge the financial support of the Government of
Newfoundland and Labrador through the Department of Tourism,
Culture and Recreation.

We acknowledge financial support for our publishing program by the Government of
Canada and the Department of Canadian Heritage through the Canada Book Fund.

Table of Contents

Introduction

By Shelagh Rogers

MARJORIE DOYLE makes me laugh. Whether she's writing about music or about Newfoundland (her twin passions, as you shall see), Marjorie's humerus bone is so exceptionally well developed that one wonders if she's not on steroids. I know what she'd say to that—not that she's in any way predictable. No, not at all.

For instance, in the summer of 1997, my husband and I visited her beloved outport home. She ran out of the house to greet us with bone-crushing hugs and then said, "stay right where you are." She ran back inside and, for about five minutes, we heard this wheezing sound. Then her partner, Patrick, appeared at the door and waved us in. And there was Marjorie at the pump organ, belting out "Come Near at Your Peril, Canadian Wolf," also known as The Anti-Confederation Song. We had a huge laugh about this choice of "processional" for a couple of Upper Canadians. But as with all great humour, at the heart of it, there is truth. And the lyrics speak to the core of who Marjorie Doyle is: a fierce Newfoundlander.

> *... hurrah for our own native isle, Newfoundland,*
> *Not a stranger shall hold one inch of her strand;*
> *Her face turns to Britain, her back to the Gulf,*
> *Come near at your peril, Canadian Wolf!*

Would you barter the right that your fathers have won?
Your freedom transmitted from father to son
For a few thousand dollars Canadian gold
Don't let it be said that our birthright was sold.

Now, it so happens that the song was published in *Old-Time Songs and Poetry of Newfoundland* or The Gerald S. Doyle Songbook. And yes, Gerald S. is Marjorie Doyle's father, whom she writes about, lovingly and without sentimentality, in the essay "Regarding *Regarding our Father*." In part, it is about the collaboration between her and her brother John as they co-write and direct a documentary about their dad. Gerald S. Doyle was a businessman who went all over coastal Newfoundland and Labrador, supplying general stores and collecting folksongs as he went. Very significantly, on his travels, he shot 16 mm colour film of the people he encountered, going about their daily lives. These films served to preserve on celluloid the pre-Confederation lives of people in the outport and coastal communities. There are some lovely surprises in Marjorie's essay which I won't spoil here, except to say that Marjorie gets to know her father both again and for the first time.

Circles seem to intersect and overlap in the life of Marjorie Doyle. In "My Uncles Didn't Dance," we learn that even though she was "a dedicated Newfoundland nationalist, ready to walk in the parade that would lead us out of Confederation," during the summer of the 25th anniversary of that very Confederation she worked as a writer and researcher for the last Confederate Father, Joey Smallwood. This begs the question: was/is Marjorie Doyle the Mata Hari of Newfoundland?

Another episode from my long friendship with Marjorie Doyle: I was in St. John's for a week hosting my CBC Radio program *Sounds Like Canada*. I called up my pal to tell her I was busting to see her. She invited me for dinner, and I presented her with two ceramic mugs with my show's logo on them. Marjorie accepted them, but then bolted upstairs, coming back down with a thick black Magic Marker and crossed out the word Canada, writing Newfoundland in its place. "Now I can use them," she said.

It was the CBC that brought us together as colleagues in the early 1990s. We were both working in Toronto at the old Jarvis Street National Radio headquarters. I walked into the office of the daily evening concert program *Arts National* to speak with a producer and there she was, installed behind an old oak desk. The room crackled with a new energy. On first meeting, she was funny and mischievous. She was a gust of fresh air at the "corp" and I liked her immediately.

The Jarvis Street studios had once been Havergal College for Girls, named for the English poet and hymn writer Frances Ridley Havergal, who was born in 1836 and died in 1879. I mention her because, like Marjorie, she was a writer and a musician. She was also the youngest of six siblings. And that is a special and sometimes challenging place to be in the family order. In Marjorie's case, she was not only the youngest of eight, she was the only girl. And the shopping expedition on which her Sophia Loren-like mother takes her, at age 10, "a scowling lump, in a raglan," had me rolling on the floor. Suffice it to say, no one writes about mortification the way Marjorie does.

She is so availably human. Combine that humanity with a rigorous intellect, a flinty wit, and a power to observe unsparingly—

even when that lens is turned upon herself—and you have *A Doyle Reader*. This woman, whom I have seen leap up on a table as a mouse scuttered across a kitchen room floor, takes on the Government of Canada, the anti-sealers, and the Ministry of Fisheries and Oceans *sans peur*. *A Doyle Reader* is a pleasure. I can hear that voice that I so loved listening to when she hosted *That Time of the Night* on CBC Radio. Reading this collection is like being with a good friend, someone who tells you stories you can identify with, someone who challenges you to think differently about things, someone who makes you LOL. But it's deeper than that because there is also the other LOL: lots of love.

No need to "come near at your peril." Plunge in anywhere and enjoy.

Immaterial Girl, and Girl's Mother

THE TAXI pulls up to a street corner in downtown Toronto. A woman in her 40s emerges. Her hair and ensemble suggest she's emulating Jackie Kennedy, or perhaps competing. She wears a camel hair coat carefully, carelessly open to reveal the tight skirt of a kelly green suit, cut to the knee. Her shoes are sleek and jewelled. She's stunning. As she leaves the car, she tosses the cabbie a wad of money and a dazzling smile. She heads for the revolving door of the grand department store when something else tumbles out of the cab, like a forgotten package. It's a scowling lump, in a raglan. It's 10 years old. Our annual shopping expedition has begun.

It is not likely I will ever be required to attend the Oscars, but *supposing* I won best actress or got asked there as the date of … well, whomever. There I'd be on that indoor-outdoor carpet squeezed into a wraparound low-slung high-arsed velour hankie. Or draped in a pink sheet or strapped into a plaid bandana because after a thousand hours held hostage in the fitting room, I seize up around the fields of fashion. I stand bereft, outside the fence, searching hopelessly for a gap I can sneak through.

The mission to outfit me in my mother's image and likeness began young. Water Street in my town was lined with homey shops and small department stores, but my mother sought exotica. She settled on Toronto—Simpson's with its classy elevators and a bustling cafeteria that offered food and respite for soldiers depleted by the shopping wars. We would idle around briefly glancing at furnishings and bedding, then set up camp in the horror chamber: the children's department. Glamour-mother and gawk-girl settled in for the day.

Saleswomen probably wondered why my mother nattered at me in an excitable monologue when clearly I was mute. I stood silent, my face inscrutable as a Swiss guard at a pope's funeral, my posture a paradigm of resistance, as if a sandwich board hung over me advertising trouble. Mother ferreted through racks and shelves, piling garments in heaps outside the dressing room. Play clothes, Sunday clothes, straw bonnets with wide ribbons and elastic under the chin. Lime green pedal-pushers with matching striped top. Nova Scotia tartan suit and pillbox hat. A purple skort. I was stoic, like a martyr being stoned, stiff as the tin man without his oil. My arms and legs were pushed and pulled, the clerks labouring as if dressing a corpse. Every five minutes I was nudged out of the cubicle and presented to an audience of thousands—bored clerks from other departments, and probably neighbouring shops, wandering by for the yearly spectacle of tireless mother and tired child. Pre-teens, tweens, teens—the ritual endured. My mother remained convinced that, with time and money, she could make me a girly girl, winsome even. She could lift me from my natural habitat of dorkdom and deposit me gently into the kingdom of cool—her cool. But I remained a conscientious objector in a small, private war.

I still panic in dress shops, I mean women's apparel boutiques, like Charlotte's Chic Showroom or Emily's Emporium. I slink in, an impostor. Sniggering salesclerks smirk: *she's* in here? Their condescension wafts into my pores, like perverse aromatherapy;

every sniff weakens me. Around me the confident bop to Abba or other upbeat minstrels appropriated to urge spending. What I hear from the sound system in flashing aural neon is: *no room at the inn.*

Fallen arches. Check. Dropped shoulder. Check. White owl glasses and scrunched nose from excessive sneezing. Check, check. It is true that my arches are fallen, but not so fallen that I deserved orthopedic boots at the age of eight. But in this one area my mother's determination to upgrade me to cute was shoved aside in favour of a larger protectiveness, encouraged by zealous doctors. My schoolmates' blue-and-white saddle oxfords seemed dainty ballet slippers by comparison. Yes, at five, I had tipped out of the back of the rocking chair and broken my nose, but a skewed visage, a slight tilt in the mouth, a crooked smile—sure, the Irish call it charming. In photos my eyes are cast down and to the right as if I am fascinated by a mouse that's nibbling the photographer's shoes. I look guilty. At a sale of work in our school auditorium in grammar school, I'd been guzzling an Orange Crush when someone elbowed me, knocking the squat bottle into my front teeth. The missing chip from my front left bicuspid added to the facial tilt and the downcast eyes shout: SLY. I was a good kid, but the photos never got it right. The truth is my head doesn't sit right on my neck. Or the head and neck ensemble don't quite fit the shoulders.

I gaze in wonder at those photos now, trying to see what my mother saw: a challenge, an obligation, a work-in-progress? Or just a piece of work.

I once paraded along a catwalk, at a Grade 9 fashion show to raise money for the foreign missions; participation was compulsory. I hid behind a wide umbrella and slunk out in my beige raglan, like a miniature Colombo. My classmates, dressed in hot pants and red vinyl go-go boots, were less conspicuous. Catcalls, whistles, and thunderous applause from the boys sent up from the neighbouring school sounded torturous but were nothing compared with the startling silence of 1,000 unruly lads turned mute at the sight of me. I walked the slow mile from stage right to stage left, then collapsed into the welcome blackness of backstage.

I was a closet person, convinced from birth that the route to invisibility was disguise. I felt silly in girly wear, but had I donned it, I would have been painted into the backdrop of girlhood. Perhaps because I lived in a house with all boys, and because fires of defiance never stopped smouldering between mother and me, I picked a wardrobe I believed inconspicuous. I had a slavish fascination with a boy in my brother's class. For years I wore brown corduroy trousers, a red blazer, and a green-and-red striped tie. Whenever I was asked my name, I answered, "Danny Williams." Years later when yon Danny became the hero premier, I hung by the phone, certain there was some role for me to play. (No calls to date.)

What had happened? What had transpired in the nursery at St. Clare's Mercy Hospital? What had happened that Ann Marie Murphy could strut about shamelessly, that Donna Keough could prance in clipped short steps in sexy high heels, that Glenda Coveyduck could, with a snotty toss of her head, settle her hair into perfection? Where was I when the fairy dust was sprinkled on them—out for a feeding?

I squirm around women who whine that they're hired for their looks. I once got hired in a phone call and fired when I showed up. On the phone I was bright and perky, just what they were looking for in a hostess for visiting mainland conventioneers. I swaggered in and 10 minutes later slunk out. I'd worn my funeral clothes, the only dressy outfit I had in hippiedom—grey skirt, white blouse, and black heels I kept spilling out of. They could have handled it with diplomacy: You don't speak Japanese? Didn't we mention we were looking for someone a little older/younger/taller/shorter? Someone who can whistle while reciting epic poetry.

In my own personal stations of the cross, number four was the corner of Prescott and Gower. There sat Gladys's Beauty Parlour, where every Friday my mother entered—comely, fetching—and left looking more so. Occasionally on a Saturday I would be toted along for a special do, say, before a brother's wedding. It's not likely my mother requested Wave Humps mixed with Frizz or Tufted Tease, and if you peruse the magazines of the day you won't find those styles, but the camera never lies. In high school, classes were filled up with teens with glossy, thick shoulder-length hair, straight or softly curled. Check out my yearbook picture—there's a hole above my name in the school library copy, but maybe you could borrow one elsewhere; you'll recognize me, suffering under a coiffure best described as CrimpKnit Soufflé.

I don't know what occupies most brides an hour before their wedding, but I was thumping out the *Poet and Peasant Overture* arranged for piano duet with—well, I'll tell you frankly, with the groom. And if we could have gone our whole lives sitting at the keyboard, I mightn't have needed a second crack at marriage. If there's one thing to avoid in life, it's a wedding day. Why such fuss over the wedding *night*? At that point, you've been released from the tyranny of flounce, girdle, and teeny shoes; the veil's been cut into tiny pieces. (Agreed: I overreacted.) The trauma is the wedding *day*, finding oneself wrapped in a floor-length gauze bandage, head veiled, inching up that long lonesome aisle like a fake white nun. From the choir loft high above me came long glorious oboe lines soaring, floating. I had a fancy to run up and offer to play for the service. If only I could have been an usher, or someone taking up collection. Was there no role for me besides this? Eyes fixed on me as if I were lumbering up the aisle at Halloween disguised as a pumpkin or a Christmas tree, wide mocking eyes gaping at this foreigner: their old pal cut out of her jeans, workboots, peace hat, and poncho and stuffed into this costume from the new country of married. To please Ma.

"C'mon, Marj, tell us the most memorable moment of your wedding day?" young romantics in the family ask.

"Oh, gee." I smile demurely. "Nice girls never tell."

Okay, I'll tell. It was in the car riding to the church, that moment of wonderment that I had allowed myself to be strapped into this outfit, and the second later when my left hand wrestled the right to keep it from ripping off the veil.

My brothers, who had not been similarly swaddled on their wedding days, remained sweet, supportive.

"How you doing, Marj? How're you holding up?"

"Fine, b'ys. Number one."

And minutes later, arriving at the church, looking up to see the resplendent mother of the bride at the top of the steps, the moment when the petrified daughter looks for a last-minute reassuring pat. She said not a word, but I was reassured. I swallowed and entered the church, suspicions confirmed: I was ugly as sin and looked a proper gawk.

I'd been living in the country, three hours from town, and had no phone. Every few days my neighbour would climb the lane to my house.

"There's a message to call your mother," he'd announce, as if it were quite normal. Then, as it to spare me shame in front of friends, he'd whisper, "I think you're due for another fitting."

Six hours return trip for three hours in the bridal salon, a large sunny showroom bustling with teams of mother-daughter, sisters, and best friends all joshing and teasing. Not us. My mother's commitment to reconstruct me had been elevated to higher standards, appropriate to nuptials. Mrs. Mullins, pins in mouth, knelt in front of me during the summit on hemline—Mrs. Mullins, another in the long line of clerks, tailors, and beauticians who tsked, tutted, and muttered sympathies to the generous mother of the ungrateful child.

"She's useless." My mother's head would flick toward me as she regaled passing trade with anecdotes of fittings and failings. She helped the staff poke and prod me as I stood fast, still draped in the now frayed sandwich board of resistance. Then the serious campaign. Personally, I saw the wedding gown as an attention-getting device; I preferred a less showy raiment. My brother had handed down a dark blue pullover—US navy issue, given him by his girlfriend's father. I knew I could make it up the aisle if I was at least partly covered up, and that thick wool sweater over my gown would do nicely. I won the makeup skirmish but mother won the war. Four days later a snow-white bride shuffled up the aisle.

The next time I got married, I searched the town for a seamstress with a secret fitting room, and found one. I don't know who her clients are, but she operates a clandestine tailoring clinic in the privacy of her basement, and she takes nocturnal appointments. To enter her quarters, you have to slink around an alley and rap at a low back door. No showroom, no loitering size-eight brides rolling their smug eyes, no fancy-pants bridesmaids. A mother-free zone.

She measured me and handed over a slip with the numbers I needed to purchase material. The next day I strode into a fabric shop.

"I'd like six yards of wedding dress, please," I began, handing over the numbers and a pattern. "Something simple."

"This fabric's not possible with that bias," the cocky assistant was pleased to announce. After much talk of darts, seams, and swatches, I fumbled, losing ground. She remained poised, until she finally twigged: *You're the bride?*

Those self-help books on the mother-daughter mire babble about discussion, healing, honesty. Didn't happen to us that way. We just grew old, so old a mother and so old a daughter that the early conflicts faded. Some barricade collapsed, leaving a small space for peace. When my mother was told she had a wool allergy, she needed a new wardrobe, but no longer had the fuel to face the shops. On my visits I started bringing in a cotton sweater here, a T-shirt there, till one day I looked in her closet and couldn't tell it from mine: fleece vests, plaid flannel shirts, Indian tie-dyed skirts. She'd lost height, she'd lost a leg, and her remaining foot was in jeopardy; she hadn't worn a shoe in 10 years. Stylish footwear now consisted of the sexiest designer socks I could track down, worn one at a time. She didn't go out much anymore, but still fussed over fashion. When she was invited to my or my brothers' houses for family dinners, our concerns were logistics: the weather, the right vehicle, who'll help with the steps? She'd leave those trivialities to us and wheel around her room, pondering what to wear. Every few months I was deputized to a makeup department. My mother's list was not easy for a paleface like me to decipher; eventually, after complicated conversations with patient saleswomen, I'd head back to the Home with a stash of Marcel powder (translucent, light, loose, not caked), new puffs, lipsticks, and other accoutrements that have yet to grease my face. When I visited my mother then, I'd amble in, grateful to be spared the adjudication of my hair and costume. Perhaps she couldn't see as well. Perhaps …

In any event, I'd open her closet door, suggest a colourful blouse or bright sweater. I'd make sure the makeup was stored in a drawer where she'd remember it. And I never left until she looked beautiful.

Newfoundland Quarterly, Spring 2010

Tender Ladies

I DON'T KNOW how old I was the day Our Lady of Fatima steamed into St. John's harbour. The caption on the photo says 1901, but that can't be—I can see her *so* clearly. Skeptics say it was an iceberg loosely suggesting a woman; others say the picture is doctored. That muddle of fact and fiction I can't explain. I only know I saw her. She was ice-white and cool, and had the bearing of a mediatrix. That she sailed on icebergs had not been made clear to me, but I knew who she was.

I knew her from a childhood pilgrimage. My mother had taken me to many holy places, and the Portuguese village of Fatima was one. I became ill there—ill at the thought of those three little kids being boiled in oil. I'd known this story for years, but now it took on a certain immediacy. There we were, standing in the very town where the mayor had interrogated and tortured the child martyrs. They'd reported that while minding sheep in the meadows around Fatima, the Blessed Virgin Mary had appeared and given them a secret message: "Pray the rosary for the overthrow of communism." The Mayor, presumably of communist leanings, tried to scare them into retracting by hanging them over a cauldron of boiling oil, dipping them in, inch by inch. Or so went the story in our reader. They were prepared to die for their faith, we were told, not like us—selfish Newfoundlanders trying to sneak chocolate during Lent.

Our Lady of Fatima had returned to St. John's in the spring of 1955, this time sailing through the Narrows aboard the *Gil Eannes*, the hospital ship of the Portuguese fishing fleet. Was I present on that cool May day, raised up on my father's shoulders to watch the grand spectacle, or is this, too, constructed memory? She disembarked at the naval dock into a waiting crowd of 4,000 Portuguese fishermen and most of St. John's. She was petite now, and had a delicate face with fine features. She'd travelled the rough Atlantic seas in the ship's chapel, and looked none the worse for wear. This smaller, sweeter plaster Lady was eased onto a portable altar and hoisted onto the shoulders of Portuguese men, some wearing suit jackets, some dressed in their fishing uniform of plaid shirts and rubber boots. They left the wharf and crushed into the crowded streets of St. John's. More fishermen, carrying tall staffs with lighted lanterns, clustered around the altar like an informal honour guard. This Mediterranean procession in an Irish Catholic town wound its way up steep hills to the Cathedral of St. John the Baptist. Inside the church, ringing richly now with robust Marian hymns, the proud gift of thanks was delivered to the Catholic community of St. John's. For hundreds of years, Portuguese vessels had sailed into port for refuge from storms, to stock up on supplies, or to offer leave to their men during the long voyages fishing cod on the Grand Banks. A symbol of this quiet cultural mingling had been sought, and found.

The statue became the centrepiece of a grotto that includes two young kerchiefed girls and a shepherd boy, the startled children from the Fatima meadow. They kneel in front of an immaculate woman who's draped in flowing robes that fall to the top of her toes, exposing bare feet. If you had visited the shrine in later years, you would have observed, kneeling behind the Portuguese children, a bank of kids in navy pleated uniforms and colourful bandanas. That would be us, lured there by a fascination with child martyrs, the rare sight of sheep in a holy shrine, and by the gentle lady.

The church was the far border of my prescribed childhood world. I was free to roam the back alleys, streets, and lanes of a defined quadrant between our convent, attached to the church, and home. Walking to and from school, we tried to scare each other—threatening sightings of the neighbourhood's perilous characters: Bucky King, Nina, Orvil, Silly Willy. The names sent shivers through us. And we would dart up side streets and hide if someone yelled a warning of gang invasion: The Ivanies! The Wheelers! *The Portuguese!*

We pretended to be terrified, although, unlike most kids in town, we were well used to these foreign seamen, mixing up with them in Mom Collins's shop. The shop was en route from the harbour to my street, Carpasian Road. Soon after their boats arrived in port, the fishermen—stir-crazy from shipboard confinement—would face the steep climb up Prescott Street, stroll out Monkstown Road, and descend Johnny's Hill to St. Pat's Ball Field, across the road from my house. There they played endless hours of soccer, in bare feet. We would sit in the meadow above the field and watch. We'd take off our shoes and socks to see if we could stand the cold. We'd dare and double dare each other to run around in naked feet, but no one could. This was not a playground in the American Midwest on a summer's day; this was St. John's—soggy, slushy, damp St. John's in May or June. We knew they were hardy; often when they played soccer on the wharf, one of them ended up diving into the harbour to retrieve a stray ball from unappealing, frigid waters. When the men had exhausted themselves on the soccer field, they'd hike back to port, calling in again at Mom Collins's shop.

The shop filled the corner at Monkstown Road and Maxse Street in the east end of town and was the centre of brisk juvenile commerce. My entire disposable income, maybe 25 cents a week, was spent there, though for all the bull's-eyes, licorice, and jawbreakers procured over the years I never forked out more than a nickel at a time. It was a small clapboard structure painted that prevailing downtown St. John's colour: a rich homey green. The store was so cramped it might have been built around Mom Collins, as if someone had grabbed a cluster of children, a few shelves of candy, and hammered up walls. To the right of the door was a window that took up most of the storefront. If she wasn't busy serving, Mom Collins kept watch on the passing world. We spent no time considering her larger life—home? family? How had she come by her sobriquet? She was ancient, a short woman barely poking up a foot higher than the counter. Her shop wasn't bustling with flirting teens and jostling bucks like Power's hangout up near the high school. It was out of the loop, on its own, a tiny commercial centre in an old neighbourhood that combined stately wooden homes and row houses. We wriggled through the narrow doorway, shifting and twisting to accommodate our lumpy bookbags. Mom Collins's entire custom was convent schoolgirls buying candies and jacks, and idle schoolboys buying marbles and yo-yos. Was it a groc and conf selling milk and other things neighbours might need? I never saw a grown-up in there. Except the Portuguese.

They were swarthy, stocky, curly-haired, dressed in rough

sweaters and faded plaid shirts. They reeked of the exotica of European cigarettes and were always in an uproar—or so it sounded to our untutored ears. What did they buy? I don't remember them buying much. We kids were tedious and predictable clientele; even our shopping hours, lunchtime and immediately after school, were unvarying. Mom Collins was suitably indifferent to us. But the ambience changed instantly when the Portuguese squeezed in. They'd loll about, carrying on a running discourse as we conducted business around them. We'd dodge under them, plunk our coins on the counter, and mumble our demands. We knew the prices of our purchases and added up our own sums. Mom Collins handled our requests without a word, a silent ballet of trade carried on inside a larger communication. Had she learned a smattering of Portuguese? Or was she just charmed by the company of these lively, funny men—the only adults she ever saw? She had a warm smile, saved for their arrival. They lit her up, spread mischief all over her, these homeless boys who travelled thousands of miles from family for half the year, to fish.

Like childhood, the Portuguese have vanished, at least from my life. Little trace of them remains in this town and, where the shop used to be, a lone bench sits on a patch of grass. There should be a plaque to those men from Oporto, Lisbon, perhaps even Fatima. I'm tempted to hammer up a sign myself: In memory of a tender link between Portugal and Newfoundland. Or erect a secular shrine to the ancient.

Who knows? Perhaps on a quiet street corner in Oporto, or in a meadow near Fatima, such a plaque, or plaster lady, exists.

Newfoundland Quarterly, Winter 2007

Holy Mother, and Holy Mother Church

MY MOTHER had a fancy for things ecclesiastical. That I was never made to crawl to Compostela or carry a cross on Good Friday are the wonders of my childhood. I did make pilgrimages to the shrines of Our Lady of Fatima in Portugal and Our Lady of Lourdes in France, with a practice romp through Ste. Anne de Beaupré in Quebec. We attended Mass and received the sacrament of Communion 364 days of the year—on Good Friday, by some liturgical peculiarity, it was not available. And every time our small bums touched the seat of the car, we recited "Three Hail Marys for a safe journey," throwing in aspirations, invocations, and ejaculations, in acknowledgment of St. Christopher, patron saint of travellers at that time.

At home, we knelt in our den night after night and prayed the family rosary—a long, lovely mumble of repeated prayers divided into five sections and dressed up with imaginative titles: *The Fifth Glorious Mystery: The Crowning of Our Lady as Queen of Angels and Saints.* Or, *The Second Sorrowful Mystery: The Scourging at the Pillar.* If I had friends over, they were co-opted into the rite. A childhood photo shows five girlfriends and me—we're about 12 years old—kneeling in a circle around my seated mother, praying. If you walked into a house today and caught children on their knees with magic beads roped around their fingers, chanting, you'd call the authorities and report a cult. Older brothers, even when they were teenagers, never got out the door to a hockey game or on a date until the rosary was finished. Gangly, awkward teenage boys slouched and resentfully "led" a mystery. Mystery, indeed.

Our house was elegant, uncluttered, but some religious icons were present—a crucifix over the bed in each bedroom, and copies of that trick picture of the Sacred Heart, where, if you look at the chalice, you see God's Head, or you look at God's Head and see a chalice, or ... Anyway, one of those Figure Ground things. We had, too, a standard issue picture of Our Mother of Perpetual Help—starlet of benediction, eponymous founder of devotions, and patroness of the Redemptorist Order.

My mother's penchant for the church didn't stop at prayer and ritual. It crawled out into a larger world and embraced two specialties: real estate transactions and motor vehicle accidents— she refused to be party to either, if there wasn't a clerical collar involved.

In my childhood nuns didn't drive. They had a car and driver for the few times they ventured out—say, to visit hospitals. When I was in Grade 7, my mother called me aside and announced she had something to tell me "in the strictest confidence." I was half afraid of my mother and her tendency toward formality, even with me, a little kid. The news was serious and I was commanded to hold it secret.

"Reverend Mother is learning to drive ..."

She might as well have said Reverend Mother was joining the Rolling Stones. It is difficult to explain the drama of this statement, the impossibility, the incongruity of it, the way my mind could not comprehend it—Reverend Mother sitting behind the wheel of the car! Reverend Mother, whom I'd only ever seen in a pew or behind a desk. I had never seen a nun outside the holy triangle of church-convent-school—except the odd pair going to O'Mara Martin's drugstore or exiting the doctor's office next door. I came out of the reverie of this astonishing news to hear her conclude:

"… and I'm going to teach her."

More terrifying news blew into my world a few weeks later when my mother rushed into the kitchen.

"We had an accident!" I was brought further into their intrigue. Nothing serious—they'd hit a commercial wire fence in an industrial lot on Logy Bay Road. My mother had hauled Reverend Mother over to the passenger seat and plunked herself down behind the wheel; there she sat, ready to take the blame. I can't remember the fallout in terms of police or insurance, but I seem to remember before my mother's next confession a detailed explanation of the theology behind the varieties of lies: calumny, white lies, lies of omission—and the ones you had to tell to keep a nun out of jail.

My mother loved conspiracies against authority: at border crossings she steadfastly refused to admit she was Canadian. She confounded customs officers, resisting their efforts to make her say the C word.

"I was born in Argentia, I am a Newfoundlander," she would repeat in a monotone, as if she'd been trained in spy school. Crossing into East Germany at the Berlin Wall, she terrified us children by concealing wads of American traveller's cheques under the crook of her arm. At another border she helped my Arizona cousins smuggle illegal Mexican firecrackers called roman candles. I wasn't really worried; I was far too Catholic for a phrase like roman candle to frighten me.

Perhaps it was the thrill of that incident with Reverend Mother that attracted my mother to a fascination with vehicular encounters of the clerical kind, because ever after she'd only participate in an accident if it involved the church. One day my brother called me from the emergency department at St. Clare's Hospital. He'd been summoned there by a friend who, coming out of Mass at the Basilica, had witnessed my mother rev up her Honda Civic and, in what appeared to have been an ambitious Mario Andretti manoeuvre, aim for the concrete steps of the neighbouring convent. She avoided a spectacular crash by hanging a fast left, two quick rights, and a final whoosh. There she sat, listing about 70 degrees, squeezed into a narrow alley between convent and church—a space in which you'd have trouble storing a wheelbarrow. When we inspected the scene later, it looked as if a helicopter had lowered the vehicle on a cable and eased it on its side into this tiny crack. The matter remains a mystery. A force had overtaken her foot, she said, gluing it and the accelerator pedal to the floor. Known facts: my mother survived without injury, the crime scene was a holy place, and, if she had perished, she would have travelled directly to heaven—no Purgatory stopover—as she was fresh from Holy Communion.

On another occasion she ended up on a tiny triangular island that divided two streams of traffic near our house. That in itself is not significant, but this spot was 50 yards in front of a Jesuit rectory. Less spectacular, but equally intriguing for episcopal connections, was an accident at the intersection of Bonaventure and Elizabeth Avenues, again only a minute from our home, the day before my brother's wedding. A minor accident, but it fulfilled the requirements: the car struck was owned and operated by the Christian Brothers. And lest by now you are thinking every car in St. John's is driven by a cleric, let me hasten to say the town is filled up with laity, heretics, and Protestants. She never hit one of them.

We spent our summers at Hogan's Pond, about 10 miles from St. John's. It's now a dormitory community filled with commuters, but in those years it was "the country," remote from urban life. On the last day of school in mid-June, we loaded up the Jeep, bumped our way for an hour or more over treacherous gravel roads, found our house at the bottom of a hilly, overgrown lane, and settled in until Labour Day. The property had a brick barbecue, a bunkhouse for my older brothers, its own generator, a park-size swing set, three motorboats, and a raft we could swim to and dive off. My mother named it Marianella.

What does it mean? Playmates, even grown-ups, would ask. Had we an Italian ancestor hanging off the family tree? Mainlanders assumed it was Gaelic, and locals thought us grand.

No, we'd rattle off the way kids do when they spill prized information. It's the birthplace of Alphonsus Liguori. Dummy, we'd add, if we were talking to a kid our age. We'd toss out his name as if he were a famous movie star, and to not know of him suggested a deficiency.

But even most devoted Catholics would not know Alphonsus Liguori was the founder of an order of priests known as the *Congregatio Sanctissimi Redemptoris*—Congregation of the Most Holy Redeemer. These priests, whose names carried the tag C.Ss.R., were called Redemptorists. In Newfoundland, they were known as missionaries hired to come and scare people during

Lent. The faithful flocked to these lengthy sermons, known as Missions: Married Women's Mission on Monday night, Married Men's on Tuesday, Single Men's Mission Wednesday night, and Single Women's Thursday. The devil, it seems, wore assorted guises, his costume determined by the potential sinner's gender and marital status. In any event, celibate missionaries strode to the altar in long flowing robes and dished out a scary brew of advice and fear to huge silent congregations. The sermons reminded parishioners it was a good idea not to stray from the fold.

The Redemptorists were stationed in Newfoundland in a few places. We knew of their Whitbourne mission, where they plunked themselves down in territory thick with Protestants and tried to combat the spread of heresy. Three or four priests lived there, with women housekeepers, and went out by day proselytizing to outlying areas where Anglicans and Methodists were rampant and newer varieties of churches were sprouting up. The Redemptorists, mostly mainlanders posted to Newfoundland for a few years, didn't have family around. They were befriended by a stunning, smart, wealthy widow: Our Mother.

When my mother wanted to sell Marianella years later, she didn't approach a real estate agent or advertise in the newspaper. She likely mentioned it to the Redemptorists, who must have declined, then drove to the rectory of the Jesuits, an order of priests newly arrived from "Canada." She dangled. They bit. Sold to the Jesuits, who handed her a cheque for half the price and a postdated one for the balance.

This business of relinquishing property only if it were to be converted into sacred quarters was not new. We'd been down that delicate, private road. Our city home, where we lived the rest of the year, was a large house on a beautiful wide avenue leading from the older to the newer part of town. It was called Grassy Knap, a secular title bestowed on the place before my mother's time. As older brothers left to marry—and enter the seminary—the house grew lonesome, the property scary. My mother ordered the demolition of one wing in an effort to make the place cozier and more manageable, but it was still too big; in time she decided to sell. The idea came to her one Sunday afternoon when we were sitting in the convent parlour at the Presentation Motherhouse visiting Mother Ursula, the bursar of the order. My mother was regaling her with the earthly delights of this centre-city Eden. She smiled a charming smile and said: "*You* should buy it."

I, a child, looked up, startled. Nuns didn't buy things. They were born and raised in convents, and remained there till they died. They had no money, owned no property—except more convents.

Mother Ursula laughed, but my mother persisted.

"Grassy Knap. It would be perfect. A convent with your own grounds and walkways, privacy, solitude, a retreat house," my mother enthused, describing the dream sanctuary of a religious order.

I don't remember how long negotiations lasted. The landscaped property—with its chestnut and lilac trees, lawns, meadows, pastures, and vegetable gardens in the middle of St. John's would have been snatched up by any clever developer or romantic homeowner, but it didn't reach the open market, and not a whiff of the news circulated around town. It was a secret deal known only by my mother, the nuns, my brothers, and me: 11 years old and marvelling that 1) nuns had money; 2) my house was going to become a convent; and 3) Sister Benigna would be sleeping in my bed.

"The beautiful thing is," my mother kept telling me over the next few weeks, "Mass will be offered there *every day*." No normal child could get excited over that prospect, but I could. Mass, every day, in my house. *Ohmygod*.

One day soon after, our much-loved childhood home passed out of our family and into consecrated hands. Sold to the Presentation nuns, preserving intact our crazy connection to Holy Mother Church.

Yet my mother did not have the fear and unconditional respect many Newfoundlanders had of the church and the clergy. She was used to priests. They were our guests, safe companions for a beguiling widow who didn't want to marry again but who basked in the pleasure of dressing up for men, entertaining them, dining and sharing a cocktail. Priests were demystified in our household. They used our cars and Jeep, borrowed our summer house, stayed overnight when visiting.

We were several degrees at least removed from normal. For us, a treat was not a family movie pass, but a plenary indulgence— we lucked in by happening on Pope Paul VI's first public blessing in St. Peter's Square. On my 11th birthday, which fell that year on Holy Thursday, my special present was to be brought to the intensive care ward of the hospital and allowed a sighting of the failing Father Clair Johnson. I don't know what the visit did for him, but the terrifying tubes and medical machinery haunted my sleep for weeks. The area was plastered with signs of "No admittance," "Family only," and "One visitor at a time." We broke through these barriers, we the chosen ones, and hung out with priests. Other kids were getting skates for their birthday, or school rings or electric curlers.

"What'd ya get for your birthday?"

"I got to go see … I saw … See, Father Cl …"

"What?"

"Oh, books and things."

We had our own priest. He worked as a missionary—his beat was a stretch of seriously Protestant shore in Trinity Bay—but in his free time he hung out with us. He was smart, well-read, and made my mother happy. They fought over Scrabble, traded hot Catholic novels, like *The Shoes of the Fisherman* and *Morte d'Urban*, and talked endlessly about Cardinal Spellman and President Kennedy. The trouble with having your own priest is you can never escape Mass, not even in summer—a potentially expansive respite from the rigours of those early rises. We would drive out Thorburn Road toward town and stop at a one-room school. Father had the key. He would set up a temporary altar on the teacher's desk, my brothers would be the altar boys, and my mother and I would sit in the front desks. It was very much like playing Mass, which my friends and I often did as, being girls, we never got to be altar boys. With grown-ups participating, the ritual was weird—falling fuzzily between a genuine sacrament and a toy Mass.

Having a portable priest meant we had our own confessor. If you think this is a good thing, picture sitting in the dining room—we called it a refectory—playing crazy eights or Go Fish one minute, and the next kneeling before your opponent, separated by an imaginary screen, owning up to your sins. It kept cards clean.

Morning Mass, nightly rosary, three Hail Marys every time we hopped in the car, benediction, vespers, brothers in the seminary, and our own priest. How was there time for anything else? And, in the midst of all this, twice a day, every day, we'd down tools and plunge into The Angelus. You could be in the middle of a game of alleys but when the clock struck noon or 6 p.m., you'd switch over like a train moving tracks. One minute you'd be saying to your brother, "gimme a bite of your Popsicle," and next you'd be rushing out: "*The Angel of the Lord declared unto Mary.*"

"Go get your own," he'd snap back. "*And she conceived of the Holy Ghost.*"

"*Behold the Handmaid of the Lord*—they're all gone."

"*Be it done unto me according to Thy Word*—tough luck."

"*And the Word was made Flesh*—c'mon b'y, one lick."

"Ouch," we winced, our heads smacking as we bounced up from the requisite genuflection.

"*And dwelt amongst us*," he'd wrap up. "And if you go up to Reid's, gimme a Coke."

Through the open kitchen window, we'd hear our mother's concluding "*Amen*"—and the jingle of car keys.

Newfoundland Quarterly, Spring 2013

Child Traveller

WE'LL SAVE the cow money and go, my mother said.

We weren't farmers, but we kept two cows whose milk was worth cash. For years this money was faithfully stowed in an account marked "E," along with the baby bonus cheques. (Our mother ignored this Canadian endowment because we were anti-confederate.) Then, one Sunday afternoon in the spring of 1963, my brothers and I were summoned to a dining-room table cluttered with pictures of the Eiffel Tower, the crown jewels, and the masterpieces of the Louvre. There were postcards of great cathedrals, Venetian gondolas, and paths that meandered along the Rhine and the Arno. There were a globe, foreign dictionaries, and a weighty book, *Ancient and Modern Marvels*. The time had come for our marathon trek through Europe.

I was 10 and hated it already.

There was no ambiguity in my mother's vision. A young widow and three kids, we would be fearless voyageurs, making our way in any town. Itineraries and reservations were dismissed as restrictive; tours and packages were for the less imaginative. We would tackle the great cities of Paris and Rome, navigating the streets with our maps and our wits. We would seek out the tiniest pueblos of Spain and knock on doors until we found a room for the night. We would shop in the markets, picnic by rivers, walk through the canvas of Monet's *Le Déjeuner sur l'Herbe*. A life-changing cultural experience, my mother enthused, seeing before her a team of junior aesthetes. But I had already encountered the highest art: I'd seen a girl in Grade 6 skip Double Dutch.

We dressed to travel, lest somebody label us scruffy Newfoundlanders. Three seersucker dresses were folded into my suitcase, along with shoes with heels and a mysterious junior undergarment. (I might develop early and we wouldn't have the vocabulary to track down necessities in a foreign country.) Hats to wear in church were collapsed and jammed in, along with rollers, in case we couldn't find beauty parlours. My mother was glamorous and I, perhaps in rebellion, was a refractory tomboy. Travelling about in nylons and bonnets, I would be touring Europe in drag.

We boarded the SS *Homeric* at Montreal in early June. As we set out for the French port of Le Havre, most passengers stayed on deck, waving to family and friends. We four huddled together, my mother beaming. As the city's skyline began to fade, my last hopes went with it. For weeks I had tried to will myself into measles or mumps, appendicitis even; alas, I was in top form.

I was a kid not meant to travel. I wanted to be home at night with the Bobbsey Twins, sneaking out of bed, opening the window and freezing myself for the pleasure of crawling back under the covers and reading more. By day, I was flat out. I had a two-gun holster. I made my own bows and whittled my own arrows for cowboys and Indians. I had a tiny Red-Rose-tea album in which I was busily pasting cards, like hockey cards, of birds I saw in the garden. I hitched a wagon behind my bike and kept a rigorous schedule delivering empty milk bottles to imaginary customers all over our 8-acre property. There were climbing spikes that needed to be nailed higher in the chestnut tree, and there were hours of pond swimming and boating to pack into the short Newfoundland summer. All this and more gone, as we left land behind.

My brothers disappeared on the voyage, except for meals. They were considered old enough to hang out on their own, doing what I never knew. That left us with a crowd of men in Bermuda shorts and white shoes—at home we called them mainlanders—who scuffed along the deck with what looked like window poles from my school, pushing pucks. Dutifully, I endured shuffleboard so my mother would have company. The activities schedule moved us from the deck to the lounge for "compulsory" Italian lessons, which ended each day with an American couple, tipsy at 10 a.m., trying to squeak out Neapolitan songs. Every morning after the last doubtful notes of *Volare*, I was sent to youth prison, somewhere in the hold of the ship. This was meant to be a recreation program, but the fun eluded me. There's a photo from the last day of the voyage, one of those "deals" in which an unctuous photographer snaps your picture "with no obligation" and then nags you into buying it for about US$50. The Greek, Italian, and Spanish kids might have been picked for this voyage for their beauty: olive skin, black eyes, glossy thick hair. They look as if they understand their cultures are superior, know their countries boast tombs and treasures sought by all travellers. They are proud and sure of themselves, like pillars of the Acropolis. With freckles, red hair, fake curls, and the wrong clothes, I look like I've been airlifted from a birthday party for dorks and dropped into a gathering of European children modelling designer play clothes. I'm scowling. In fact, of all the pictures taken that summer, there's only one in which I don't look like a hostage who's lost hope. The photo was taken in a restaurant in Rome. We'd been escorted there by an Irish priest who wanted to spend the evening flirting with our good-looking mother. The others are smiling. I'm too busy to pose, tucked into the only familiar food that I saw in the whole three months: a steak.

My Newfoundland childhood had failed to prepare me for the challenges of European cuisine: *Wiener schnitzel, fondue, escargot, goulash, borscht, viande séchée.*

Even spaghetti was unrecognizable, the Italians surprisingly unfamiliar with the Newfoundland preparation. Breakfast— previously taken for granted—required a maturity I could not muster. There was an embargo on toast, it seemed. All that was on offer were buns so hard we called them bones, and long crusty loaves we'd caught sight of travelling through soot and diesel, sticking out of the backs of scooters. The day I broke down and cried for a real breakfast, my family took me seriously. My brothers pored over their pocket dictionaries and my mother— undaunted by language barriers—drew upon her wiles, but to no avail. On the entire European continent there was not now—nor had there ever been—a bowl of Sugar Pops.

More foreign and intolerable than the food was the heat, generated by a blazing, merciless sun. Was the wind blowing fresh at home unable to reach across the ocean? No whiff of a breeze to move the heavy still air—just the noxious diesel fumes of trucks and trains. And crowds. Crowds meant competition for space; every venture onto and off a bus was a battle, and all "attractions" had queues. I developed a lifelong dread of lineups. No pavilion, no play or musical, no opera or concert, *nothing* has tempted me since to queue—except the time I lined up, not so much to see Bob Dylan as to see Bob Dylan *in St. John's*.

It wasn't long before *pensiones* lost their appeal. I wanted a hotel with an elevator and an elevator man; better still, a motel with a pool. One of those nice Howard Johnson's, decorated all orange and blue and with a kid menu, somewhere you could get Chicken-in-a-Basket or Shirley Temple cocktails. But there were no hotels or motels on our journey—we scoffed at these, and sought out *garni* and inns. We scarcely saw the inside of a car, opting instead for buses, trams, trolleys, the Metro in Paris, the tube in London, funicular when necessary. We did take taxis in London after we saw *My Fair Lady*, where Eliza Doolittle pulls up in front of Henry Higgins's house and says to the butler: "Tell 'm I come in a taxi." To be in London not driving around in those wonderful black cabs would be like boycotting *gelato* in Florence.

We travelled almost exclusively by train. With Eurail passes, we could hop on and off trains at will—as much as a mother, three children, and eight suitcases can be said to hop—without advance notice or reservation. The perfect way to do Europe, unless you're 10 and wearing heels. My mother's idea was to travel on a budget and see how the Europeans really lived. You would not find us in the dining cars with Hercule Poirot; we were ennobling ourselves on the railway platforms, grabbing hard rolls, strong cheese, and warm flat *agua*. We never stopped long, trying to cover as much territory as we could during the life of the pass. It was a summer of countless hours spent in railway cars engaged in bitter conversations with a pet monkey I'd adopted from the Munich zoo. At 10, I was too old for an imaginary companion, but my girlhood was one of retarded development. (When I was 17, I was at a formal ball, waltzing closely with my date; I was lost in a reverie of delight over a practical joke I'd played earlier at school, when something wet and unpleasant occurred near my mouth. It took a few more bars of "Bridge over Troubled Water" for me to process my first kiss.)

I wasn't—or hadn't been—a fearful child, but the journey became a string of tiny nightmares. In Ireland, I was hung out over the side of Blarney Castle an inch too far, a second too long, trying to plant my lips on that cold Irish bull's-eye. New horrors awaited in Paris when the platform quaked—no, *we* quaked as the platform shook when we stood on the second level of the Eiffel Tower. (The fear of heights is still with me: a few years ago on a steep trail that climbs above the ocean on the west coast of Newfoundland, my companions were astonished when I fell to my knees, turned around, and *crawled* back down.) At Madame Tussauds waxworks in London I burst into tears when I realized my brother had made me ask directions of an embalmed policeman.

And the trip went on. Was there no end to the sights to be seen? The *Pietà*, David, the Mona Lisa, Montmartre, Chartres, the Tower of London, the crown jewels. I trudged, begrudged, and tramped my way through the lot of it. And at any one of these precious sites, I would have sold myself into slavery for a bowl of Frosted Flakes.

Exotica and adventure craved by tourists were incomprehensible to me. Why were we over there dying of the heat lining up to see boring things when we could be home playing cowboys and Indians and driving my "3"? (A tiny motorboat with a 3-horsepower engine.) From the moment we had left Torbay airport in June until we arrived back on Labour Day weekend, I was hot, tired, and dying of thirst. If there was a television set in all of Europe, we never saw it; yet there was no tomb, tower, or Baptistry door that could make up for three months without *Leave It to Beaver.*

Our itinerary, unofficially, had a Catholic aspect. At home we were daily communicants and said the family rosary each night. Shortly into the trip, we abandoned these routines for practical reasons: four can't kneel in the squatty room of a *pensione.* As for Mass, my mother had not recovered from finding herself in a Protestant church in London (her introduction to high Anglicanism). Yet we did keep our eye out for relevant sites, places like Castel Gandolfo, an extravagant summer camp for popes, and Assisi, where St. Francis let me down: I fell about a foot off a steep path and was saved only because my 13-year-old brother, whose usual reaction to fear on my part was to laugh, sensed real danger and dragged me back.

Coming to grief in holy places seemed part of it. At Lourdes, where the sick are made well, I became sick. The magnificent shrine in the south of France stood on the spot where the young Bernadette Soubirous had "seen" the Blessed Virgin; it was the site of cures for many who then left their wheelchairs, canes, and crutches hanging around the church. We left nothing, but took away a spoon from the hotel so that my mother could continue to give me the medicine the French doctor had prescribed. (She mailed the spoon back from Ancona.) And in the Portuguese village of Fatima, I was ill again—ill at the thought of those heroic child martyrs being dipped in boiling oil by a communist mayor eager for them to retract their sighting of the Virgin Mary.

On the voyage over, we'd received the news that Pope John XXIII had died. This was a setback. The only engagement we had for the entire three-month journey was scheduled for the Vatican—we were in possession of much-coveted tickets for the beatification of a Redemptorist bishop. At 10, I took the news in my stride, although I knew my mother was keenly disappointed. Even my two brothers took it harder than one might expect of teenage boys. But they were being groomed for the Redemptorist seminary; perhaps showing up there flashing stubs from a beatification would have the same cachet as hockey tickets in a different environment. Now Rome would just be Rome, with no hoopla or privileges.

But we arrived in Rome to discover excitement: a covey of cardinals was hard at it in the Vatican, attempting to elect a new Pope. To catch out Pope-candidates and cardinals in such a pedestrian activity as an election was shattering to me. (At home in Newfoundland even the premier wasn't elected, or so I thought: Joey Smallwood was the head of state, as a matter of course, and had been since before I was born.) But here was an election being secretly conducted behind the facade of the great and mystifying Vatican! Holiness took a plunge.

We hung around St. Peter's Square, waiting, waiting, just a few hopeful tourists like ourselves, eyeing the sky for the puff of white smoke. (The ballots are burned after each vote, but when a clear winner emerges, some potion is put in the fire to make the smoke white.) The square was virtually empty, a peacefulness broken only by the odd nun scurrying across the courtyard, looking more ominous than the nuns at home. On the second day of our vigil, white smoke appeared. From behind pillars and inside doors, from all corners of the square, from walkways and ambulatories, people came. We were swarmed as eager Italians ran to get closer to be able to hear the cardinal who would appear in a distant balcony and announce the name. There were shouts of *"Habemus Papa!"* ("We have a Pope!") and suddenly we were swept under. I grabbed my brothers' hands and held tight. When the crush was over, our mother had vanished. We climbed statues and peered out over the crowd, but it was hopeless; there were thousands of people in the square. Well trained, we swallowed our panic long enough to kneel at the appropriate moment as Pope Paul VI gave his first public blessing. We were kids but we knew the value of a plenary indulgence. But what should have been a moment in time, marked by a sense of history and holiness, found me instead hot as hell, and desperate for that elusive Coke. We ended up finding our mother by asking directions to a part of the Vatican where a Newfoundland monsignor lived; she'd had the same thought.

And after Rome there was Venice, glorious Venice. We would travel the canals in water taxis and gondolas, me getting sick as we wended our way through the rotting garbage floating on both sides of us. And now, nearly 40 years later, I go to wakes on the first day, before the flowers wilt, lest an olfactory madeleine transport me to the foul Venetian canals and make me sick. More troubles on the Adriatic when a plateful of fresh cherries—confounding anyway as they bore no resemblance to the Avon filling—brought on a seasickness so visceral I can't listen to Verdi's *Otello* without feeling queasy in the opening scene.

And on we went, traipsing across the continent. In East Germany heavily armed soldiers boarded the train and checked our papers. We saw the Berlin Wall and its gatehouse, which my mother passed through with her left arm held tightly to her side, hiding the traveller's cheques she feared might be taken from her. Brussels, Amsterdam, Nice, Seville, Milan, and through it all, nothing made an impression. In my mother's journal, if you crossed out all references to me and substituted another name, you would think the family was travelling with an invalid with special dietary needs who had to be carted from place to place. In the entire three months, there is only one moment in which I seem to have perked up and taken note. It was in a souvenir shop in Rome where the customer ahead of us was a nun who bought 24 pairs of rosary beads. My mother's diary records: "Marjie amazed."

Geist, Fall 2007

Bridging Troubled Waters

I STILL call it suntan lotion. I wear laced shoes with lifts, even on a beach. I swim with sunglasses on. And while the beautiful people are pirouetting to disco-volleyball, I'm in the dork's end of the beach with the bookish crowd, hidden under a Tilley hat. The white Cuban sun beats down on me as I lose myself in Africa with Paul Theroux, relieved his sexual vanity has expired and I can read *Dark Star Safari* without the usual Leporello litany of the Don's conquests. I'm harmless enough, armed only with my room key and a second book for when the first one runs out. Harmless, *except*, according to American journalists, I'm "supporting an immoral regime that enslaves its people."

I spent my childhood on my knees praying to defeat the Kremlin. At 10, I'd happened on Fatima. I'd seen the meadow where the Virgin Mary handed three Portuguese kids a secret letter. Secret, but word got out: "Pray the rosary for the overthrow of communism." So we did. I was like a power nailer firing steady rounds of Hail Marys at that barricade of evil. When the Berlin Wall fell, it looked like the work of a wrecking ball, but those with eyes to see could find among the rubble shards of my prayers fervently intoned, then rushed, skimmed over, yawned through— the quality of prayer declining as the fervour of childhood waned.

It is shocking then that, having waged that long war, I can

lounge on a beach, drink warm punch, and bask in the heady air of pure communism. I can hand out American $1 bills and contribute to the collective Canadian irritation of America by supporting a corrupt repressive regime.

The day after I booked my flight to Cuba, I got a phone call from a stranger (I live in a small town) asking me if I would carry a package from him to a worker in a resort on Varadero beach. Could I *what*? Isn't the first rule of smart travel, don't carry strange packages into foreign lands? Perhaps it was cash; perhaps the currency of condescension—toiletries, combs, and trinkets that Internet gossipers instruct you to bring because "the people will love you for it."

I declined the courier gig, but I knew what it meant. A slow, steady parade of grateful Newfoundlanders files into the Cuban sun, year round. Fifteen years ago, an announcement of travel to Cuba raised eyebrows. Do they keep you on the compound? a friend asked. Nervous relatives warned you'd never see home again; worse, you'd be turned pink. These days? There's no formal agreement, no embassies or attachés, but the islands of Cuba and Newfoundland are tentatively bridging across Atlantic waters. First cautiously, now eagerly, wan, desperate Newfoundlanders flee 8-foot snowdrifts and biting winds—or elusive summers—to ease themselves into Cuban warmth. The package I'd been asked to transport might have been photos, books, cash, or something a departing Newfoundlander identified as a useful gift to a new friend. Inside resorts and outside government pacts, these oddball twins are bonding.

Why wouldn't they fall in as comfortable allies? Both societies grew out of small open boats, fishing, and a muddle of religion, poverty, and colonialism. Their economies, traditionally, were tied to the sea. Island-dwellers connect easily. Both societies elude the press; they are studied, summed up, and reported on by earnest observers who seldom get it right. Both have known the sweetness of being small island nations. And, as the crow flies, we're neighbours.

I'm a reluctant photographer. When I remember to tote a camera, I forget to use it. On those rare occasions when a roll of 36 comes back from processing, there'll be three Christmases and the wedding of someone who, a few snaps earlier, is a kindergarten grad. My partner is equally indifferent to the contemporary compulsion to digitize a moment and launch it into cyberspace before the smile fades. That's why I panicked when he shot out from under his cabana, rooted through our beach bag, tripped over my lounge chair, and beat it into the water, running along the edge of the sand, holding his camera high above the splashing. He stopped within a few feet of a small open boat with two fishermen on board, an old man and a boy about 15. A large net straddled the boat. The boy jumped into the water. The old man remained in the boat and picked up the net. It was open-mouthed, circular, and bordered with small leads. He stashed a small part of the weighted net between his teeth and spread his arms wide, grabbing two more pieces. Balancing himself carefully and holding two ends of the net, he brought his right arm back toward his left, stretching as far as he could, all the while munching the leads between his teeth like a seamstress juggling pins. He rocked his body gently until the swinging motion felt right. Then, with the skill of an athlete and the grace of a dancer he released the ballooning net far into the sea, his mouth spitting out its netting at the same time as his hands. I watched the delicate choreography.

My partner huffed his way back.

"My father and I—," he panted. He'd just seen a cast net for the first time since childhood when he and his father had fished the frigid waters of Conception Bay for capelin, precious fertilizer for a subsistence potato garden.

I carried on watching: two men, small open boat, a net, a hunt for food they will eat themselves. Elemental, direct, primal. They were in and out of the sea, as if water and air are the same to them. They were scantily dressed. Their black hair and deep brown skin made a stark, dark beauty against the white sand and the perfect azure sea. Two men in an open boat would look different in Newfoundland waters. A fisherman, even in July, is bundled in bulky layers and foul-weather wear. A licence number would be painted in large black digits on the outside of his vessel. The fisherman would be catching this species, not that, and he would take the measure of the fish to see if its size was acceptable. The skiff would be loaded with gear deemed compulsory by Fisheries and Oceans and Transport Canada. Officers patrol the bays in small rubber Zodiacs. They are authorized to pull over a vessel for a safety inspection, asking to see whistle, bailer, anchor, fire extinguisher, flashlight, compass, spare parts, gas and extra gas, oars, rope, axe, re-boarding device (newspeak for ladder), and more. They don't ask to see your underwear *yet*, but that may come. (A friendly check, to see if it's thermal.) On the wharf, when the fisherman returns to shore, Dockside Monitors (an invention of Orwell?), clipboard in hand, assist the federal government. It's like arriving at the end of the supermarket checkout to find the police rooting through your groceries. Not all surveillance is so transparent. Government personnel occasionally hide on headlands using infrared glasses to spy on fishermen after dark. The crime could be catching one cod. The punishment can be confiscation of cod, confiscation of vessel and gear, a fine. At Varadero, I watched the man and boy, unencumbered. They were close to Hemingway's Santiago of 50 years ago. I know it is illusion on my part, simplification, ignorance that makes this scene look so casual, so free.

How am I to puzzle out the "truth" of Cuba? How am I to penetrate this hot, sandy island? I want to sport my new Fidel T-shirt, but is that a slap in the face to Cubans who don't appreciate being kept at home? Is it like visiting a prisoner and saying: Nice big yard—you must love it in here?

At the lobby bar one night, handsome, suave Enrique asked: "Where you from?"

"Terra Noba." I learned my Spanish in Bar*the*lona; in addition to the lisp, I picked up the b/v confusion peculiar to the Spanish.

"You know Mount Pearrrhl?"

That's like being in Bulgaria and when you say you're Canadian the Bulgarian asks if you know Etobicoke. Enrique knew the sleepy suburb of Mount Pearl through his erstwhile *novia* (girlfriend) from there, someone who'd come on a package tour and left with a promise. She'd been back and forth, but ultimately the relationship had ended. No matter, he was married now to a doctor in Ontario (another package tour) whom he'd be joining once the papers came through. I'm going slightly crazy. I'm on vacation in Cuba having a conversation about the streets of Mount Pearl. Then, in the dining room one night, I hear a familiar song. Newfoundland music is not imported into Cuba, but it can be carried down and left as a gift.

Cuban images stir in my brain: a younger me, half-stoned, watching the crazy television show in which Joey Smallwood and an eccentric millionaire sit in a television studio on opposite sides of an empty chair. Their meandering conversation is peppered with speculation about why their invited guest has failed to appear. *Waiting for Fidel*, a Newfoundland cult film, was my introduction to the dark, exotic, scary island of communist Cuba—by the early 1970s I hadn't travelled far from the nightly rosary.

On Internet websites travellers offer insider tips to fellow tourists. Do this, don't do that; expect this, not that.

"Staff were efficient but not overly friendly."

"Maids don't speak unless you speak first." Petulant, or what? Don't they like cleaning toilets? That the Cuban's English may be limited and the foreigner's Spanish non-existent seems to elude the tourist.

"They smile, but their smiles don't look genuine." The rating of resorts and services spills over into a review of the country, an adjudication of attitudes from which tourists extrapolate levels of personal and national happiness. From similar assessments of the demeanour of front-desk clerks in downtown Toronto one might conclude Canada was a dour nation of cold young snobs.

"They don't smile, and their unhappiness looks genuine."

But who can get it right? A friend spent four months living in Havana as a student in a program of International Development. He left, no wiser about the "truth" of Cuba. Are free health care and education cancelled out by the denial of personal freedom, freedom to leave? Some foreigners argue most Cubans wouldn't leave, even if they could. I say, where's the data for that statistic?

And even if every Cuban granted the right to leave chose to remain, that's hardly the point.

"The people have nothing; they love perfumes and aromatic soaps," the Internet sages write. So you load your suitcase with junk from Wal-Mart and, for $10, you can lie on the beach feeling magnanimous, swelling with the satisfaction of membership in the club that got the good tourist tip. You come armed with the savvy of those who'd gone before. But those who've gone before should report what is coveted, *needed*, is US cash.* I strolled into a Dollar Store, where the only accepted currency is American dollars. The Cuban peseta *no existe* inside these four walls. There are side counters with local perfumes and *coral negro* jewelry, but the brisk trade is local. Here Cubans can purchase fridges and washing machines, but only with US dollars. I stood in front of a stocky white fridge and thought of the American $1 bills I had handed out as tips. How long would it take for the waiter in my resort—who's really an unemployed vet—to bring home this basic appliance? How long to buy a bicycle, much needed for the long hot journeys to and from work? A mountain of $1 bills looms in my mind. I see a second mountain of toothpaste and bath soap that tourists lug to Cuba each year because "that's what the people want."

"Helllllllo," a tourist gushes at Conchita, today's breakfast star. Chefs perform in the buffet lines, even at breakfast. Omelets are custom-made. You can trouble yourself to learn a few Spanish words—like *queso* (cheese) or *jamón* (ham)—or you can articulate the word loudly in an English unrecognizable to them. Or you can point.

* This has changed; the US dollar is no longer legal tender in Cuba.

"George," *la turista* mumbles to her husband, "give her some money."

To Conchita: "We missed your smiling face yesterday." Her singsong inflection carries a hint of warning, as if she's wagging her finger at a small child saying "better not try that again." The tone changes as she repeats her low mutter: "George, slip her something." A clumsy transfer of a crumpled bill completes the scene.

I grew up with a catechism in my hand, quizzed in school by day, at home by night. So a book called *100 preguntas y respuestas sobre Cuba* fits comfortably in my hands. I like doctrine clearly laid out. Were there a parallel book of *100 questions and answers about Canada*, what might the questions be? The Cuban primer gives short answers about the flag, heroes, *analfabetos* (illiterates— there are none), and the gravest crime, treason. From a Canadian primer: Can you work for cash and hide it in your mattress? The answer is a 9,000-page income tax act. Can police officers burst into a house and terrify innocent inhabitants with impunity? Theoretically, no, but really, yes. Can you end up in jail for a crime you did not commit? Really, no, but really, yes. Canadian waters can be murky, too.

I've seen baseball twice. In Toronto at the Skydome, my eyes are pulled up to a mammoth screen where giants play a noisy game. A bellowing voice barrels nonstop from a sound system suspended from the heavens. Musical clichés are blasted, signature motifs that must mean something—an out? a strike? foul play? These are cues for us to cheer or groan. There's the stink of junk food and warm beer, and the sick drip of catsup as galoots crawl over rows of seats. My ear stings from the curses shouted past me by a disgruntled fan. On the video enlargement the instant replays smack me—wham! wham! When the pitcher throws, I wince; when the batter swings, I duck. Far below I see a tiny field where Lilliputians scurry around a grassy (fake?) diamond. Ah, *there's* the game. At the Matanzas ballpark, near Havana, baseball is still a sport, and it's acoustic. You hear the thud as the ball meets the mitt, the crack of the ball on the bat. Here, Fidel arrives without fanfare. He likes to hang out at the field. The primer boasts that 90 per cent of Cuba's successes in international sporting competitions have been since the revolution.

Cuban *pregunta*: Are players paid? Are there perks? Status? In Toronto, pitcher Roy Halladay's annual remuneration is $10 million. I've entered the Matanzas diamond free.

Canadian *pregunta*: Why would a minimum wage worker plunk down $35 at a ballpark to support a multi-millionaire?

I laze in the shade picking my way through *preguntas y respuestas*. Around me the resort gadfly flits. She's exhausted. It's her first trip out of England, and she's gathering evidence for the presentation back home of the perfect vacation. On the beach she engages in animated haggling with a *viejo*; the old man is selling wood carvings. (She'll boast she beat him down.) She poses for a photo, sprawled on the strand, teasing the waves. More photos: at the swim-up bar with the handsome *chico* from the recreation team, in the weight room with the handsome trainer. She's not vacationing in Cuba, exactly; she's vacationing in that expansive, no-name generic country of Resort. Cuba is the backdrop for all-she-can-drink drinking, all-she-can-eat eating, and flirting.

I, too, slide into Cuba for the sun and the sand, carrying no curiosity, no eagerness to learn. An easel hangs in the lobby with daily temptations: fly here, drive there, rent this or that. Make a cigar. Visit a church. Shop in old Havana; see the port, the fort. I am a resistant tourist, committed to indolence; nothing lures me off the beach. I use the country: the beach as a beach, the translucent water for a perfect swim. I gaze at the hospitable sea and, lone bone in the dying day, linger, watch breathless as the burnt gold sun creeps across a vast canvas of sea and sky, deepening, bloodying, darkening until, as I remain staring, it is gone.

I have been to Cuba seven times. Each time I become more profoundly involved with the country—my drinks get stronger, my naps get longer. The front-desk clerk was engaged to a young woman from my home, and one night I danced in the sultry open air, under black jewelled skies, to a Newfoundland waltz. I rarely poke my nose outside "the compound," yet Cuba has tumbled into my life. My Cuban library is growing: Ivonne Lamazares's *The Sugar Island*, Alina Fernandez's *Castro's Daughter, An Exile's Memoir of Cuba*, Carlos Eire's *Waiting for Snow in Havana*. On my first visit to Guardalavaca, I heard an odd fluttering pitch from a low bush. I crept over and coopied, silent, watching a bird the length of my middle finger "sing" with its hovering wings. My nightshirt is a grey rag now, the neckband loose and torn, but the fading hummingbird is still identifiable. I've learned Cuban music from the musicians who roam the restaurants singing their seductive songs.

When my guardian angel flew off some years ago, her spot was seized eagerly by an exacting bore with a one-word vocabulary. *Los musicos* stop at my table and sing "*Hasta Siempre*," the stirring tribute to the heroic Che Guevara. I join in: "We will follow along and with Fidel we say to you, 'Until Always, *Comandante.*'"

"Really?" probes my hovering skeptic. I squirm. But *la banda* is smiling at me, and I at them as, over another clumsy cash transfer, we sing in perfect harmony.

Inside the picture of the guilty traveller to Cuba, the greedy tourist supporting a repressive regime is a fledgling Cuban-Newfoundland network. I love this new dance between these foundlings, a pairing of people centred on the sea. Cuba's a beach, Newfoundland a rock. Cuba's hot or pleasantly warm; Newfoundland's cold, or colder, and for a handful of days, modestly, teasingly warm. I watch Cubans move in and out of the water as we go in and out of the rooms of a house—casually, not saying ok we're in the dining room and now let's brace ourselves for the kitchen. Here we prepare with attitude as we plunge into the water or crawl out again, knowing that way, too, lies shivering and discomfort.

My partner emerged from the Divorce Wars with a small valise in his right hand containing toothbrush, underwear, and a worn copy of *Moby Dick*. Under his left arm, he'd managed to tuck a painting of the Virgin by Cuba's Rene Portocarrero. It hangs in our front hall. She's not the Virgin of my childhood; no folds of crepe paper draping her, and she's not standing on a dais. She is, though, the power, the mediatrix who, with my help, knocked down the Berlin Wall. A remaining fortress is Cuba. Am I unwittingly invoking her to bash down one more barrier? I have no Hail Marys left. My hope is that the political barricade around Cuba will crumble into the sea, smashed this time not by a battery of invocations but by time, by a change in leadership, by quiet and consistent political pressure from the home governments of the tourists: Germany, England, Spain, France, Canada, and Newfoundland. Near the Cuban Virgin in my house is a Tish Holland serigraph, *Casting for Caplin*, which reminds me as much of Cuba now as it does of my own island.

The piano bar was empty one night, the pianist home sick. My partner suggested I play, just for us. A few people trickled in and, well, it was not a lie of commission, just omission; patrons, mostly new arrivals straggling in from squatty planes saw nothing suspicious in the musician at the ivories. Only the truly paranoid would arrive in a resort and say, yes, but is the bartender really a bartender? I'd been playing Cuban music, trying to get down the tunes for "*Hasta Siempre*" and "*Besame Mucho*." My keyboard skills could cut the job and my fledgling Spanish, flawed to the Cuban ear, was convincing to a foreigner. A tourist sidled up to me and articulating slowly and speaking loudly, asked, "Can you play any English music?"

I was about to start "Land of Hope and Glory," pleased to meet a fan of Elgar, when he said, "Like Simon and Garfunkel or Billy Joel?" I answered with the opening bars of "Sounds of Silence."

"Hello darkness, my old friend," he crooned and I played along. Photos were snapped. The caption, I assume, read: Cuban pianist who could play English.

Descant, Fall 2006

Homage to Barcelona

BARCELONA. No wonder it's madness, with four million people trying to squeeze into a comparatively tiny space. Here is a city emerging from a long dictatorship; that may explain the resentment toward any law that hints at impinging on individual rights. Or it may be a deep-rooted love of anarchy that goes back to long before Franco. In any event, there is a pervasive scorn for anything that inconveniences the individual for the collective good. A request to a neighbour to lower his stereo at 4 a.m. is greeted with outrage. Not only is this a denial of basic rights but where's the problem? You're free to play your stereo louder and later tomorrow night. And so it goes.

Take parking, for example.

The accepted system—which works, sort of—is to park where you want, when you want. If you find yourself hemmed in on all sides, you simply sit in your car and blow your horn until the guilty parties come forth. Except they're not guilty parties here. No apology; not even a glance or nod is exchanged. It's a problem, then, only for a foreigner who's reluctant to add more decibels to what must surely be the noisiest city on earth. An *extranjera* doesn't feel comfortable sitting with her hand glued to the horn for, say, 20 minutes. But this is a city in which volume is a virtue. How noisy is it? Imagine that city council is working on your street with a jackhammer, there's a house under construction next door, every youngster on the street has just been given a ghetto blaster and a motorcycle, and the muffler's gone on your car, your neighbour's car, and your neighbour's neighbour's car. That would be a quiet moment in Barcelona.

Louder is better, the motto seems to be, and everyone does his best to live up to it. On the street there's the continual blare of horns as cars park and unpark, and there are thousands of muffler-less scooters. In the *bodegas* (cafés or bars), there are TV sets, gambling machines, and coffee grinders that seem especially designed to rub your nerves raw. I retreat to my flat in grateful anticipation of a few moments' solitude with my electric piano. But even with top volume I still hear only the neighbour's radio, the schoolchildren playing next to my terrace, and the Andalusian singing floating down seven flights from the maid upstairs. I begin to accompany her—it's good practice for my ear—but eventually I give up. I don't know then that the real noise doesn't begin until the hot summer nights, when everyone eats (late, as the Spanish do) on their terraces. There'll then be countless sleepless nights with a clashing of cutlery that sounds like one big swordfight. In retrospect, this will seem a quiet time.

So you can't be in and you can't be out. Maybe the parks are quiet, and there'll be grass, a precious commodity in a dry climate. I think there are two patches: one is in a little English garden tucked inside the walled protectorate of the British Consulate; the other is here, in the park. Your poor hardened toes are just beginning to sink into the soft stuff when the shrill whistle of the Guardia Civil suggests that grass is only to be seen. One look at his hat, more persuasive than his weapons, and concrete doesn't seem so bad. When you've reached the noise saturation level, you head back to your apartment building and descend three floors below sea level. But you can only hide out so long in a parking garage.

So you climb around the jungle city, crossing six lanes of traffic to get your morning croissant at the neighbourhood bakery. Not a bad life, really. It's just that when you find yourself in a crowd of 50 waiting to brace the crossing, you suddenly notice there's an equal number ready to attack from the other side. Experience in the Metro has taught you a law of physics you didn't know before—two people can occupy the same place at the same time. Or, at least, there's a strong conviction here to that effect. With the vague hope that tackle football can be learned on the job, you hunch your shoulders, duck, and charge. The lucky ones make it to the other side. If you had a *peseta* for every person you touched and tackled along the way, you could even buy a second croissant—chocolate, maybe. So you return from the battlefield for a little reprieve, sit, and contemplate. The thought of the fruits and vegetables finally wins out, and off you go again.

And here, in the *frutería*, you come face to face with one of the peculiar ironies of Barcelona. In the midst of a city of madness and anarchy, there is an orderliness that would challenge a Swiss. You enter the store and call out, who's last? I, someone answers, and you fix your eyes on her, anxious not to miss your turn. It would be easy to in the scramble—there are two or three shopkeepers continually calling, who's next? who's next? and you've also got your responsibility to shout "I" to the person who enters the store after you. If by chance you do miss your turn, there's nothing for it but to leave and enter again. As with most things, this system is learned the hard way. It's easy for a foreigner to violate the order.

War erupts, in two languages. In Catalan (the language of this region) and Castellano (Spanish) there are cries of: this lady was before that old man, that old man was before this young girl, that handsome young one was before that woman there, I was before her, she was before him, he was before me ... The shopkeepers remain silent. Whose fault is this anyway? the customers are shouting. Somewhere in the corner is a quiet Newfoundlander admiring the size of the avocados and noting that lettuce *is* green. *La inglesa*, they finally notice, *es la inglesa*. Ah well, so the Brits take the rap.

The sense of propriety continues when you are served. A kilo of oranges, half a kilo of bananas, and four apples, you rush to tell her. You quickly learn all requests are ignored except the first. After your oranges are brought from the bin, weighed, priced, and placed ceremoniously in your shopping basket, you're asked, what more? And on it goes, item by item. If you want one apple and one orange and they are next to each other in the bins, you learn to tell only about the apple at first. The apple is carried to the scale, priced, and deposited. Then, and only then, is the subject of the orange addressed. This sense of concentrated devotion to the activity is even more pronounced at the butcher shop, where you go to buy, say, a rabbit. You wait at least 20 minutes to be served, but then you are given the butcher's fullest attention; she will carefully and wholeheartedly do anything you want with the poor little thing in front of you. The butchers are usually raised on a rostrum behind the counter; this, and the fact that all eyes are on her, turn the activity into a show. The requests are thorough and varied: a chicken or rabbit will be skinned, boned, quartered, shredded, turned into patties, prepared for stew, the liver for this, the kidneys for that; every conceivable direction is given. By the time you get your little rabbit home, you're intimate with it. Underneath this procedure in all the shops there is the continuous rhythm of: *Ultimo? Yo. Quien es? Qué más? Algo más?* Who's next? What more? Something more? You eventually get the hang of the system. You don't waste much time worrying about your performance in the *frutería* as another reality of Barcelona hits you on the way home. This is the sight of the countless poor rummaging through the huge dumpsters that stand on every corner. You try to convince yourself first that they're scrounging for odds and ends, but before long you have to face it: they are hunting for food. This, and all the begging in Barcelona, is something you never get used to. Poverty and unemployment manifest themselves here in various ways. There are the hundreds of homeless who huddle in shop doorways at night, carefully guarding their few possessions—usually more scraps of thin clothing. Then there are the men, in their 20s and 30s, who frequent the public plazas. Some sit on the sidewalks with a sign placed in front of them: I am hungry, I have no work, I have six children. Others kneel and hang the same sign around their necks, a posture that is disturbing as much for its self-abasement as for the confused sense of guilt it seems to suggest. And it's not uncommon for a pair of small boys to enter the Metro. One stands still and cries out a prepared speech: my mother is sick, my father has no work, I have seven brothers and sisters, we are hungry. The other walks through the car with his hand cupped. At the next station, they hurry onto the next car, and so they pass the day. Sometimes one boy will have an accordion; he can't play it (he's barely big enough to carry it), but he opens and closes it and some sort of wail comes out. One night, walking up the famed Ramblas, I literally tripped over a baby bottle, nipple up. I looked down to find a young woman sitting on the pavement with an infant in her arms and a baby (maybe 10 months older?) lying across her lap. She and others are there every night, right in the path of Barcelona's wealthiest, the opera patrons pouring out of the opulent Liceo, dressed in furs it's never cold enough to wear. There is money in this city, a lot of it. Money is made, and money is saved. (A local joke says that copper wire was invented by two Catalans, fighting over a *peseta*.) The Catalans pride themselves on their industry and are always careful to make the distinction between themselves and the Spanish.

Yes, indeed, the Catalans are separatist. When my choir was in France performing with a local choir, the conductor asked at the first rehearsal, where is the French choir? and they identified themselves. A moment later, where is the Spanish choir? I hauled my hand back just in time. Silence. After the conductor repeated his question, a strong, clear voice announced: *Nous sommes Catalans.*

In Barcelona, a Spaniard means someone from Spain; this is Catalunya. It's easy to understand the Catalan position. During the *dictadura* (the Franco regime of about 35 years), their language and culture were suppressed. Most Catalans over a certain age can't read or write their language. In an office, for example, in which nearly everyone is Catalan, the memos and correspondence will inevitably be in Spanish. On the other hand, there are some Catalans (usually women who've never worked outside the home) who haven't spoken Spanish since their school days. A few women whom I saw regularly told me they never speak Spanish. They did it with me as a concession, although I was asked more than once why I was learning Spanish when I wasn't living in Spain.

The Catalans are proud of their language and insist that foreigners learn it. But they are a warm and indulgent people and they'll never refuse to speak Spanish. In fact, they'll tolerate any mistake and struggle to understand the wildest attempt at pronunciation. (It's only when you cross the border to France that you remember what linguistic snobbery is—if you're one shade off one vowel sound in an otherwise respectable sentence, they look at you uncomprehendingly, making you wonder if you've slipped into some rare Beothuk dialect.) Nevertheless, trying to learn Spanish in a Catalan city is not easy. When I first arrived in Barcelona, I heard enough vaguely familiar sounds to think I could fall back on my old church Latin, but relationships are somewhat limited when all you can do is confess and praise.

Barcelona, you thought: skiing trips to Andorra, weekends in the Pyrenees, and wonderful *menus del día* (those three-course meals, with wine, offered for $5 at midday in all restaurants), sitting on the Ramblas sipping cool *sangría* and nibbling on *tapas* it takes you months to work off. Yes, that too is life in Barcelona, and the joys of the city are not to be underestimated, as the initiated well know. But the pleasure pales when your status turns from tourist to livyer.

After a few months home to breathe clean air and bask in quiet (cold quiet, I might add), I returned to the insanity known as Barcelona. Before there was time to be defeated by the city's noisy madness, I realized what it was that had made my time there enriching. It isn't easy to move from an island like Newfoundland to a city as dense as Barcelona (second to Calcutta, they say), but when you break down the dreaded crowds and seek out the individuals, you find a generous, tolerant, humane people. And to add to their charm, some of them now speak broken English with traces of a St. John's accent.

"So, you come back," a former student smiles at me over lunch.

"Yes," I say, delighted that we can now converse at a comfortable level of English. This is the student who always told me on rainy days to put my umbrella in the chicken. (It was one of those attractive mistakes I never had the heart to correct, knowing that my Spanish was just as colourful.)

"I say me today, how is doing Marjorie?" she tells me warmly.

"I've been thinking about you, too," I respond.

She raises her cup of champagne in a welcome-back toast and I follow suit.

"Cheese," she smiles at me, proudly.

"Cheese," I echo, my teaching days over.

Evening Telegram, March 18, 1989

A Day in the Life
of a Languishing Teacher

I WALK into the office rested and fresh on a Monday morning ready for another week's battle.

"Here is Marjorie now," and "here is the teacher," I hear all around me in Spanish and Catalan. These are eager students, studying to get ahead in their work. And it's always fun to learn a foreign language. (Isn't it?)

"I come now," a student says to me in the outer office.

"I'm coming now," I correct.

"Yes, I come now too," he smiles. And I leave it at that. We're not even in the classroom yet.

Anyway, today will go smoothly. Just a quick drill to refresh their memories after the weekend. Something simple, like the past tense.

"What did you do last night?" I ask.

"I watched the dishes."

Watched them do what? I just stop myself from asking.

"And what did you do?" I ask another.

"I washed TV."

I'm not giving up yet—it's only Monday. But I'll go for fluidity today rather than accuracy. You don't want to inhibit them too much.

"What did you have for dinner last night?"

"Fried kitchen," a student tells me earnestly, falling into one of the common Spanish-English mistakes. When I arrived at one office on rainy days, I would always be directed to the kitchen and told to put my umbrella in the chicken.

It seems like the past tense is not going too well, and they all look a bit sleepy. We've had too much *cava* (Spanish champagne) on the weekend. So, I ease up. They know the present tense and they know all about question forms and auxiliaries. I know they know 'cause I taught them.

"Do you like coffee?"

"Yes, I like."

"Do you like cava?"

"Yes, I like."

I keep going around the room. Surely someone will remember. Finally, "Do you like wine?"

"Yes, I do."

Saints be praised, someone remembers "do."

A general round of drill now that we're all refreshed on "do."

Do you like ... Yes, I do ... Do you like, Yes I do ... until one student suddenly brings us all up short.

"Please, what is 'do'?"

What indeed. In terms of learning English, "do" is just a little less painful than "would." "Do" they remember "would"? I ask myself.

"Do you like coffee?"

"Yes, I do."

"Do you like wine?"

"Yes, I do."

"Do you like music?"

"Yes, I do."

And now, we're ready for it.

"Would you like some coffee?"

"Yes, I'd," says one smart one, sure he's winning extra points with his advanced thinking. He remembers that contractions are important.

Time for a *pausa*. We'd all like coffee by now. Yes, indeed we'd.

If you were to make a list of what brings tears fast to the eyes of a language learner, contractions would certainly be high up there. I'll, he's, we've, we'd—all highly unpopular words. Students would much prefer to say it all out, even if you tell them they sound very foreign doing so. And when they finally do accept that contractions are more desirable, their eagerness gets in the way. My name'SSSS Juan, they'll hiss at you, boasting that they know about apostrophes.

Wait till next year when they'll want their English to be at an even higher level. They'll be participating in international meetings where English is a must and promotion in their jobs depends on their command of it. And they don't want to sound foreign. But on the day when you first introduce question tags, there's a general unhappiness in the room that almost makes you feel guilty just for being associated with the English language, let alone teaching it.

You're coming, aren't you? He wasn't there, was he? She'll be there, won't she? They've said it, haven't they? It's a lovely day, isn't it? She would have gone, wouldn't she? By this time, the floor is covered with salty tears. But the sorriest day in the life of an English teacher is probably the day that "get" comes into it.

There's the "I've got" business, and "get in the car" and "I don't get it" and "she got sick" and "where did you get it?" and ...

Back to simpler drills. I let them chat among themselves for a while.

"Say me, how many childs do you have?" I hear, but this is an improvement because usually it's how many sons, the Spanish words being the same for both children and sons. There are other colourful statements, too. One man, who works for Dannon yogurt, tells a colleague that his company deals in "milky products."

Each student has particular idiosyncrasies that no amount of teaching changes. And, truth to tell, I like their way of saying things. One student who struggled hard with TH now puts it in everywhere.

"That is thrue, that is very thrue," she's saying now.

"Yes," her companion agrees. "That is the exactly problem." They heard once somewhere about "ly."

"Can you swim?" I hear one student ask another, and I know his answer will be impossible to interpret. A long time ago he got the idea that the difference between "can" and "can't" has to do with the vowel sound. So, he says can and con and only he knows which is the positive and which is the negative. No amount of suggesting that the "t" in "can't" would help does any good. He's convinced that the quality of the vowel carries the meaning. An interesting linguistic theory.

But am I laughing? No, partly because mistakes aren't funny when you're the teacher. As soon as you find yourself behind a desk with a piece of chalk in your hands, you kind of lose your normal capacity for humour. Also, I'm here struggling to learn a language, too, and my faux pas are all too fresh in my mind.

When I was living in Switzerland years ago and first learning French, I went to the post office one day to send my sister-in-law a birthday present.

"What's in the package?" asked the postmistress.

"Une corneille," I tell her, best accent I can muster up. A nice basket, too, it was.

No, she said it couldn't be a corneille. Yes I said, it most certainly was. And on it went.

"Why are you bothering to mail it?" she finally mumbled to herself as she grudgingly filled out the forms and allowed me to proceed. What a peculiar question, I thought, until humility drove me to the dictionary, where I learned that one little letter had made a world of difference. I could see her point now. If you're going to send a crow from Switzerland to Newfoundland, why bother to wrap it?

I was careful from then on, but the problems started up again when I moved to Spain years later and made another stab at learning. I was at a choir rehearsal one night chatting away with one of my colleagues. Out of the blue he suddenly leaned over and kissed me twice.

"Qué pase?" I asked him, taken aback. What's going on? (If he'd been a little younger, maybe I would have let it go.)

"I'm just giving you what you asked for," he replied, somewhat offended. I suddenly saw myself as a menace, walking around Barcelona requesting the most unlikely things. How was I passing my day?

I'm sitting here thinking all these things while I keep an ear on my students. One young girl is trying to impress the others with a description of a party she attended the night before. It must have been her first time at a dressy party. With great sweeping gestures, she moves her hands down along her body to paint a picture of the glamour of the evening.

"All the women in long dresses," she says, omitting the verb as usual. "And all the men in suitcases."

Ah, well, another day, another peseta. Time to go.

"See you tomorrow," I say, knowing that the fluidity business is over and tomorrow we're down to serious work again.

"See you, Marjorie," they say. "See you first think in the morning."

A View of Her Own, 1996

The Jacked-Up History
of Newfoundland

"The Jacked-Up History of Newfoundland" was part of The Jack Cycle, presented at the Ship Pub in St. John's, March 2011. Storytellers and writers were brought together by Chris Brookes to help forge a Newfoundland epic based on the Jack character, the hero of many Newfoundland folk tales.

I MET JACK. Yes I did. Met him on the way to the festival. And I said to him, Jack: They're going to change the name of the place. And Jack said, change the name of the place? They can't do that, Marj. You can't erase a name after 500 years. People would throng the streets, demand a referendum, clamour for a vote. You can't just announce some morning that the name of a place has been changed.

And we got up one morning and it was announced: The name of the place has been changed. And that was that. And where was Jack?

Jack was under the bushes, behind the tree, sleeping it off, gone missing. Jack was in Fort McMurray earning a living, he was at sea, at the hunt. He was in a remote university studying someone else's problems. And now here I am bi-geographed. I live in two places at one time. My DNA has been divided and where once there was one of me now there is two: I am a Newfoundlander, and Labradorian. And where was Jack when they dissected me? Same place he was when drungs and lanes and lines became loops and trails. Jack was invisible. Jack was mute.

But Jack's like the cat. He comes back.

March 31, 1999: Down at the Stadium, you know, where Mister Galen has his groc and conf, the government got up a party, a soiree I believe they called it. It was a salute, the official salute to 50 years in *Con*federation. Same night, in a house in the woods on the side of a pond just outside the city a party of patriots gathered for an alternative event. One guest sent regrets. Where could he be? Early morning strollers on the waterfront were the first to spy it: Next morning, April 1, strung across the face of the hills above the Battery looking out over the town for all to see in life-sized letters an S, M, A … *SMALLYWOOD*. Where was Jack? Resting comfortably. His work was done, he'd left his mark.

Now it came to Jack one day wandering the downtown that the most visible point of intersection today between Newfoundlanders and their history is the mermaids—those garish tarts preening around town—feigning a link between us and our past. It was Richard Whitbourne, after all, who saw them cavorting in the harbour and recorded the "fact."

And that it is mermaids keeping our history alive makes Jack uneasy. That's why he invented The Jack Test, a re-creation of the Grade 5 exam youngsters would have had in the 1960s—that one year we studied Newfoundland history—only now we're all grown up. And the test is issued by government. (Jack's got an uncle an MHA, and somehow or other Uncle Jack is in Young Jack's thrall.)

Forty-nine questions appear on the test—*49*—and you

have a lifetime to do them. Questions are available when you approach government for services or licences. You can opt to do the whole exam in one go, say when you're young applying for a driver's permit. Or you can spread it over your lifetime—amortize it—over all the moose licences and blood tests. You go for an X-ray, you can answer one question. And when you get your marriage licence—every time—you can answer two or three more. To prevent cheating or "helping out" there have to be many questions—thousands of millions and millions of thousands—and to keep crib sheets from circulating there has to be a giant computer that will spew them out randomly, and who's in charge of the computer is—well it's a giant computer so who's in charge but Jack.

Where is Jack? Jack is in The Rooms. And here's why.

The Rooms looks like a fishing premises the way the Taj Mahal looks like a dory. Sure if they hadn't named it The Rooms, people would be calling it The Glooms. And because the name stuck on, it bears no connection with the real thing; it's the perfect symbol for the gap between what is true and what is said to be true. An emblem for the fallacies and exaggerations of the record of this place. That's how it came to be that The Rooms is the repository of Newfoundland history.

The Rooms is Jack's box. It's a magic box. You can't see the contents, but it's all in there: the Newfoundland railway, the ballot box from Sally's Cove, all the ballads and poems ever written—"The Bastard" is up there. The Churchill Falls contract—that's in a little cubbyhole, tucked away, you've got to have special keys to get in and Term 29 is there. The Amulree report and the Treaty of Paris and John Guy stowed away with that hapless crowd huddled around him trying to make a go of it. (The first reality *Survivor* show.) Papering the walls of one room are portraits of famous Newfoundland politicians—that's the Mugs Gallery. On the top floor is a lovely mural of Sir Robert Bond holding in front of him, as if an offering, a little pouch of coins.

And all around the building is the Jack Statuary, or the Jackuary: all the Jacks in Newfoundland nicely sculpted in marble: Jack the Sailor, Jack Hinks, Jack Pickersgill, Jack Harris, Jack Hunt, Jack Wells, Jacks Fontaine, Jack the pro, Jack the anti, and a horizontal bronze plaque with the inscription "Up the line with *Jack*man and Green."

In the airy foyer, sitting on a huge book and writing in it with coloured pencils—pink, white, and green—and big thick markers (red and black) are all the historiographers, the scribes, the scholars. It looks like a rug or tapestry but it's a giant book. And at the end of the day, the year, the century, when they are finished, they will wrap themselves up in it, and a room will be set aside for it and it will be called the Jacked-Up History of Newfoundland. Hiding behind the Jackuary-Statuary—watching every stroke, every word, every letter, swirl and curlicue of their quills, observing all that research and thinking and writing are scientists, political scientists, members of Memorial University's Political Educators Scientists and Tautologists Society. (You may know them by their acronym: MUNPESTS.) And hovering over MUNPESTS at the very top is Jack. Jack at his best, Jack the vigilant. Because one day Jack found the wires, the mini microchips, and headsets. And he cottoned on: While the scholars toiled in obscurity on the manuscript, the MUNPESTS had a direct line to the media. And they were broadcasting, not what they were reading, not facts or knowledge, but interpretation of it—objective disinterested interpretation of it because, well, they are scientists.

In the People's paper one day the MUNPESTS announced they were bursting wide open all the mythology of Newfoundland. Jack started reading it but he got the heaves. Besides, he was never much on going to church—so sermons and finger-wagging preachers didn't sit well with him.

Jack waited for the outcry, the uproar. Silence. Then on the road one day he met an old sage. The sage explained: the population is suffering from a virulent disease: VC.

VD? Jack was alarmed.

VC—Vestiges of Colonization. Strains are found all over the world, but it's particularly healthy here, and contagious.

The symptoms, asked Jack? And the sage replied: Big ears and small mouth. You listen too much, speak too little. Others call you ill and prescribe for you. You must self-diagnose and write your own prescriptions.

But I have no knowledge, said Jack. And in his finest hour Jack understood, and that's really why he invented The Jack Test. (I was only foolin' earlier about the mermaids.) Jack decided to make up for his lowest Jack-self, times he cowered when bullying labels of xenophobic and jingoist were hurled at him. When Jack was told, if he didn't laugh at an N joke, he had no sense of humour. All those times Jack was silent or had slunk off picking berries or chasing a princess, or tormenting Peg Bearskin.

These days Jack carries a sack of yeast—to help us rise. He sprinkles a few specks on babies at birth—at the christening, sort of like a Jacktism, and every few years when we're enervated and sagging, Jack goes back and tops us up again. He figures when we don't rise up, the environment is comfy/cozy for describers and prescribers. It's a circle, a cycle, and we need a Jack-cycle to get us out of it. A jackcycle if you will, like a bicycle, and we need to mount it next time a MUNPEST says Newfoundland was on the verge of bankruptcy at the time of Confederation, mount it waving little flags that say $40 million surplus, $40 million surplus.

Suppose Newfoundland history, the whole lot of it, happened in one day. Say, for argument's sake—Regatta Day. So that the early morning gathering at the boathouse (when the committee raises the flag for the go-ahead) that's the dawn of modern history. The lone scow on the pond is the Viking ship approaching the island. And the end of history as we know it—or let us say the present moment is nightfall when the last lone townie, the Regatta aficionado, scuffs his way home, kicking at the paper chip holders and Dixie cups and crosses up through the cemetery, through the ghosts of our old country, under the neon glow of a memorial to Newfoundland's war dead—curiously dressed up like a supermarket.

And the crowds throughout the day are all the people through all the years, and the booths, well they're the shops and ships, churches and schools, mercantile organizations, unions. Well, then, on that day, that spectrum of Newfoundland history, where'd be Jack? Flitting in and out among the crowds, making mischief, outsmarting, betting on the races, and chasing the pickpockets he sees fleecing the crowd—Valdmanis, Shaheen, Squires. He lets the first two go, but there's something about Squires that galls him; Jack makes a grab for him, tries to wrestle him down, but Squires has cronies, handlers. He escapes.

At the sealing booth for 50 cents you can throw a dart at an effigy of Pamela Anderson. Jack tries, and wins a flipper pie. He's sitting outside in the shade of the bandstand, hiding. Jack's not a coward, but how do you tangle safely with the International Fund for Animal Welfare (IFAW)? He's gazing out at the pond mulling over this when Mark Walker strolls by. There was no time for thinking, no time for delay. Straight from his head came this song right away:

> *Little Jack Swiler sat for a while there eating his flipper pie.*
> *He looked out at the flotsam*
> *Thought of Paul Watson*
> *And nervously thought, dare I?*

Jack was there that night on international TV with the royal trio: King (Larry), Sir Paul, and Prince Danny, Jack whispering in Danny's ear, spurring him on while the old Beatle clung to his ice floe. Jack climbed the political throne another time, too. Now he walks to the tent—a grand marquee boasting a wide banner "*1984.*" Inside on comfy chairs sipping sherry, looking out of place in their elaborate court robes: Ritchie, Dickson, Beets, Este, McIntyre, Chounard. They're chuckling. Jack scurries round the back, listens in.

"And they thought they would win! The whole seabed! Sweet Newfinland crude indeed …"

Jack had appeared before them speaking through his medium; he'd been defeated, but he savoured the proud moment. He strides off now cheerful. "And have not will be no more. And have not will be no more, and have …" And to everyone he greets that day, he passes on his optimistic mantra, up and down the side of the lake it travelled from lips to ears and lips to ears but a word dropped here and a syllable fell there and by the end of the day, Jack's swaggering slogan had sagged and slowed and morphed and every last man Jack was muttering: "pickled in low expectations."

Jack at his finest. 9/11, when Newfoundlanders took in thousands of stranded passengers. That's Jack. Do anything for you, unless you hire him, then it's why would he want to do that for you? The most hospitable people in the world. Ask for a favour, you'll get it, but don't expect service. The diner might be closed for lunch, but no odds. The owner lives next door and he'll take you in and give you a bite of dinner. That's when Jack owns the restaurant.

The TSN nightly television program SportCentre came to Newfoundland one night to a bland, booming town on the outskirts of St. John's. The smooth anchors were up on an outdoor stage broadcasting live. As they wrapped up, someone walked up to the well-groomed trio, shoved a dead codfish under their noses and insisted they kiss it. The incident has been recorded in the Guinness Book of Records under Greatest Challenge Ever to On-Air Television Anchors in the History of the Medium. Would that Jack had rushed up, run interference, tackled the fish-man—not to preserve the anchors' aplomb—but to spare us the idiocy and the image of us projected across the nation. But Jack did not. The incident took place in Paradise. Jack, I suppose, was off in the garden having his way with the Queen.

And what was Jack about when he squirted drops of dye into the paint cans outside the freshly smartened-up building on Duckworth Street at St. John's Lane. A patriot designed his premises to sport the tricolour, but Jack got at the tins and the owner woke to find his political statement gone awry. The edifice he's left with is not quite pink, white, and green. It's like the nation itself. We want to believe, we pretend, we claim we celebrate the past but we're slightly off: Like the newly painted building, most days, most of us are coral, beige, and aqua. The old colours are fading.

June 24, 1997, in the Battery, a stone's throw from the Narrows in the cold air, on a foggy night, I stand on the doorstep of a friend's house. Sailing through the Narrows is *The Matthew*. It's the re-enactment voyage, the 500th anniversary of John Cabot's arrival in Newfoundland. Across the threshold of my host's house, he passes me a parcel. Here, he says, this turned up tonight. I open the package to find my Grade 5 textbook—source of all my understanding of Newfoundland history: From the mind of Frances Briffett to the imagination of 10-year-olds in Newfoundland in the 1960s. Not just any textbook, but mine. Inside on the flyleaf in childish scrawl my name and phone number: 90995. Passages are underlined, important passages; the underlining gets thicker. The deepening pen marks hint at the wide-eyed disbelief, the seeds of rage as the child scholar learns about fishing admirals, the 1820 whipping, King William's Act, Beaumont Hamel. When we get to 1933, the pen has poked through the page.

I glance back out at *The Matthew*, the sails, and memory stirs. I've seen the ship before, that rigging. Unbelievably, I can picture my friend on the top mast. The fog's thick outside but lifting in my brain and I see it: on stage at a pageant of Newfoundland history, John and Sebastian Cabot swinging from the ropes of a constructed set. My thespian friend was Giovanni, the brother Sebastian, my brother. The source of historical accuracy? The kid sister's textbook. It had been missing for 40 years. How had it surfaced on that particular night? Well, Jack had come over the first time on *The Matthew*. I dare say he'd stowed away for a second trip in through the Narrows.

Why Change the Name of This Province?

HERE WE go, off again to Ottawa, to change the Terms of Union. This is getting to be a habit. And if the grief and fallout from this round are anything like the last, I hate it already.

This time the issue is changing the name of the province. (The last time it concerned educational "reform.") Premier Brian Tobin and his government and the Opposition—every last man jack of them—want to change the name of the place from Newfoundland to Newfoundland and Labrador. A dramatic step, if you stop to think about it. When's the last time you heard of a province or state changing its name? And because of that thing called precedent, keep your eye on the process. Some idle soul in your province might cotton on to the idea.

Newfoundland is not an insignificant island; it's one of the largest islands in the world. It's been a nation, a colony, a dominion; its name has been around since the 1500s. Labrador is part of Newfoundland. It has been since 1763, when the coast between the St. John River and Hudson Strait was placed under the governor of Newfoundland.

A more contemporary clarification of the relationship came in 1927, when the Judicial Committee of the British Privy Council awarded a large portion of Labrador to Newfoundland. This landmark case between Newfoundland and Canada is known as the Labrador Boundary Dispute, and you can read every line of it in a 10-volume set, found in libraries and rare book collections.

It was Joey Smallwood who took the first step in the process that son-of-Smallwood now wants to pursue. In the 1960s, Joey, in an arrogant and arbitrary move, suddenly began referring to the Newfoundland government as the government of Newfoundland and Labrador. Mysteriously, government stationary was changed to reflect Mr. Smallwood's action. Soon the new name appeared on licence plates and, bit by bit, organizations bought in. You have to hand it to Joey; he invented a province. There's not a premier in Canada today who could pull it off.

You might suspect him of political expediency, but there was no demand for the change, no pressure or grassroots clamouring. Nor is there now. The population of Labrador is about 29,000. This is out of our total population of about 575,000. I can't even begin to understand the accommodation. It seems odd to change the name of a place, without good reason. If the justification is that Labrador is a separate land mass, well then, get ready for the push to rename this country. How does a passport with Canada and Newfoundland embossed on it sound to you? Reasonable?

This proposed new name is not even in keeping with the current trend to keep everything short. Our traditional abbreviation, Nfld., has been reduced to NF. That will soon become NL, because it will be only a matter of time before someone tires of the new cumbersome Newfoundland and Labrador and we will be persuaded to travel under the name NewLab. I promise you, this will come.

In the meantime, start thinking about your own corner of the country. The people of BC should get ready for the new, more inclusive province of British Columbia and Vancouver Island;

Nova Scotians will undoubtedly be happier in a place called Nova Scotia and Cape Breton. And Quebec would be remiss if it did not broaden itself. Where are you from?, you'll ask a Montrealer one day. And he'll be sure to answer: Oh, I'm from Quebec and the Magdalen Islands.

And speaking of the Québécois, would they squawk a little when Newfoundland sticks Labrador onto its name? In recent years, maps have appeared in Quebec that suggest people there don't accept the Privy Council decision. They may be less uneasy with a province called Newfoundland and Part-of-Labrador.

I'm in a hard spot here. Changing the name of this place has been approved unanimously by the House of Assembly; it remains only for the Parliament of Canada to change Term 1 of the Terms of Union. It seems strange to argue that the Parliament of Canada should veto the will of the Newfoundland legislature, but I'm arguing it anyway. Changing the name of this place after hundreds of years is a serious matter; yet it was not an issue in the recent election. And there's been no referendum.

So, here's one Newfoundlander who's asking members of Parliament to ask themselves why the name of this province should be changed. If the answer is because the people want it, remember this: The people have not been asked.

Globe and Mail, May 31, 1999

The Urge for Going

I WAS hauling myself up from Water Street to Duckworth Street the other day when I walked smack into the newest piece of St. John's graffiti. It's on a concrete wall at the top of a steep set of steps joining the two venerable streets. There's a huge map of the island painted black and a flaming red slogan sprawled across it: Free Newfoundland.

As someone who made pilgrimages as a child, I know a shrine when I see one. Clearly I'd arrived at the altar of Newfoundland nationalism. There was only one thing for it: genuflect, light a candle, and pray we're out before Quebec.

But of course you can't let on that you think like that. Not here in Newfoundland, where you're dismissed as romantic, impractical. Not there on the mainland, where the suggestion that Newfoundlanders might want to leave Confederation invites mockery. And outrage. It irritates people no end to think there's another crowd around making the "Quebec problem" worse. Better hold your tongue or Brian Tobin will have another fleet of buses on the move.

But why is that? Why is it that the Québécois are allowed to talk (shout, cry, bawl, whine) about leaving this country, and no one else is? Let someone from British Columbia dare raise the issue of that province leaving Confederation, and they're out with the stocks, eager to expose the traitor. But what completely floors the nation is when someone from this island asks: Are we on the right road staying within Canada? The collective eyes of the country roll. The unified guffaw is heard across 6,000 miles.

Surely Canadians in BC or any other province have as much human right to question their status within Confederation as do the people of Quebec. As for us, it is more natural that Newfoundlanders would open this dialogue than any other people in the country. We're an island. We were a country. And we've been in Canada less than 50 years. Think about it. In the overall history of a place, 50 years is nothing. In years to come, if we are on our own again, the period we are currently in may be summed up in a dictionary entry in a single sentence: "Newfoundland … for a short period (in the 20th century) was linked to the neighbouring country of Canada."

I'm not being disingenuous here. I'm not trying to provoke. I honestly feel we have come to such a pass in Newfoundland that not only is it not wrong to examine the path we are on but it is in fact the responsible and intelligent thing to do.

One hears a lot of talk about how to develop the economy here. I find myself increasingly thinking of simple measures that would have a huge positive impact. But they are measures more easily implemented by a country than a province. I'm sick to death of phoning a local shop only to find myself in conversation with someone from Virginia. (Yes, it really was Virginia.) And I'm tired of getting bills for local services postmarked Ontario. You've got to work hard to keep your pennies in Newfoundland.

The desire to be a country again isn't just about economics. The recent resurgence of the anti-sealing campaign by the IFAW makes one long for a strong national government that would react appropriately to these religious zealots. (Surely the baby seal has been deified by now.)

In my youth I made my annual "statement" on March 31, the date we became a province of Canada. These varying activities, designed to draw attention to the end of Newfoundland as a nation, seemed clever at the time. In my sober middle years I'm not the least bit tempted to hide out on the university campus and release balloons with political messages from the library windows. I see theatrics for what they are in politics: important, but not enough. Yet I am more convinced than ever that we should at least be asking whether we are doing the right thing to remain in Canada.

Small countries can and do work. It's true that in the 1930s we couldn't meet the payment on our debt, but that didn't have to mean the end. Our fortunes after that probably had more to do with the agenda of Great Britain than with our financial situation. During the hundreds of years we've been here, fortunes have been made and great wealth accumulated from natural resources, trade, and commerce.

There are hundreds of Newfoundlanders floating around (here, and not here) with intelligence, passion, a knowledge of our history, and an idea of how places work. Can it be so difficult to harness that talent and produce a small successful country? We have huge natural resources, and there are fewer than 600,000 of us trying to live here.

Globe and Mail, November 17, 1997

Whose Woods These Are ...

I CALL it path rage, a variation on the more familiar road rage. It reached its peak one day after a two-hour backpacking trek through deep woods—unowned woods; or if you want to think of ownership, owned by you and me. It was the sight of a cabin, walled in by cartons of empty beer bottles that unleashed an anger that had been smouldering for years. And, as if the cabin-king expecting me had planned a further act of defiance, an empty plastic Old Sam was dangling at nose level from a low branch.

A few minutes later, a second cabin came into view. This one, lodged almost on top of a fishing pool, had accoutrements: barbecue, generator, satellite dish. One can only marvel at the caravan of ATVs and their slow, steady march to create this Club Med in the deep woods. After the awe comes the rage.

The rage is three-fold. First, anger at the arrogance of the individual who's claimed as his own something that belongs to all of us. Second, the desecration of forest for indulgences unrelated to the woods. The pleasures of the woods centre around quiet, privacy, stillness, observing bird and animal life, learning and honing certain skills. You can drink and watch TV anywhere. The third tier of the anger is this: it is these cabin owners and others like them who are driving the government's agenda to further regulate and restrict life in the outdoors.

The abuser is best friend to the bureaucrat who's eagerly piling up rules. Those regulations, together with the requisite licences and restrictions, are helping solidify the wall being constructed in this province between the individual and the outdoors. Behind every new regulation making the outdoors less appealing and less accessible is a misguided, or perhaps bored, bureaucrat trying to preserve his/her job. The greater the incidence of abuse, the easier it is for government to justify new restrictions. Oh to live in a society smart enough and savvy enough to cut off the government at the pass, a place where individual and collective responsibility limit the need for regulation.

But that moment in the primordial forest behind the barrens of Western Bay was not the difficult moment. That came months later as I was hurrying through my mail, paying little attention to an unmarked manila envelope. I opened it and out fell a thickly folded map. It was a topographical map of the area I'd travelled. Accompanying it was a short letter from the provincial government asking me to mark an "x" on the spots where I'd seen the illegal cabins.

My heart raced, and my hands shook slightly. This was uncomfortably close to being involved in something secret and conspiratorial, to being, in fact, an agent of the government. And yet, I'd invited this. In an irate newspaper column written after my experience in the woods,[1] I'd boasted that if the government wanted to know where these cabins were, I'd reveal their locations. I'd meant it, or believed I did, at the time. The communication before me now was not from an idle civil servant calling my bluff; it was genuine, and it startled me to find myself so close to the policing of Newfoundland I'd suspected and loathed.

This was the moment that crystallized for me the whole

environmental problem in Newfoundland: rights and freedoms versus the need to protect the place and its beauty. I live on a teeter-totter of resentment: on one side, against every restriction placed on my relationship with the outdoors; on the other, against everyone who mars the environment, in even the smallest way. The manifestation of this is that there are days I would support a system in which every tin and bottle purchased in the province is embossed with an ID number so that when litter is found in the woods or water, the owner can be traced and penalized. I go from that extreme to knowing I will give up trouting before I will buy a permit to put my pole in the water. The resolution of this lies somewhere in the area of education or appreciation or a code of ethics so entrenched that policing is unnecessary. It has something to do with a sense of collective ownership.

It is painful to say this, but I have never once had the pleasure of fishing or camping in Newfoundland without finding bits of broken glass or a soggy carton under my foot, and I have been in many remote places.[2] Yet, just as my desire to track and expose the offenders reaches military heights, I recall the sick feeling in my stomach when I heard during the food fishery weekends that there were cod cops on the wharves, "taking down names" of who's been out and who's caught what. It was as if the Prefect of Discipline of my convent school had suddenly had her territory— and power—expanded, and we adults were reduced to standing like nervous schoolchildren, having to turn our pockets inside out to see who's got gum.

Newfoundland is one of those places where many people have a loving and intimate knowledge of the land. You can stand in a supermarket line for 10 minutes and end up having a conversation with a stranger about a particular spot in the woods or on a river. Elsewhere, the conversational connectors people call upon are places they've travelled and the ages of their kids. But in Newfoundland it is not uncommon to overhear someone saying: "You know the second pond in after you come to the bridge, when you turn off just before the dam? That clump of alders, just before the big juniper? Well, right past that, on the left, that bog. That's where the bakeapples are."

How is it, then, that not just a candy wrapper, but a washing machine or a car can be found in the backwoods? Rather than reflecting tenderness toward the land, this would seem to suggest contempt. There is no justification, but perhaps there are explanations, although one hesitates to contribute to the potentially perilous Newfoundland practice of rationalizing our failings by reciting a litany of historical woes and grievances. Nevertheless, it has to be acknowledged that our people were not rich; hand in hand with economic deprivation goes a poverty of imagination, an absence of aesthetics. Imported marketing concepts such as "clean and beautiful" don't mean much when more rudimentary tasks occupy one's mind and time. Practical concerns and a daily battle with an untamable, unpredictable sea drove the quotidian life and work. Land was seen in economic terms, for what it could yield, not as a patch of nature to be prettied up. It wasn't too long ago that in many Newfoundland communities it was possible to identify one white house (among many) by saying: the one with the tree in front.

Houses in communities were close together, on small lots. Gardens were often elsewhere, on meadows beyond or behind the community. Land was the outback, everything behind the community a resource. Wood was brought out from there, for building and for fuel. In some areas land was also a source of food such as berries, moose, and rabbit. The backwoods was a supply centre and there was nothing to suggest it wasn't infinite. It was there, it was free, it was accessible. It required nothing from you to maintain or preserve it. It was easy not to value it, like the keys to your parents' car.

On the other hand, to make sweeping generalizations about Newfoundlanders and garbage is to try to make the contemporary notion of "waste disposal" retroactively fit onto a model where it isn't appropriate. The word "recycling" and its current meaning are new and imported, but the concept is an old and familiar one in Newfoundland. As Owen Hiscock points out in his memoir of growing up on Coward's Island, Bonavista Bay, there was little or no garbage in his community.[3] Items were used and re-used, often with great ingenuity and imagination. Many Newfoundlanders are still familiar with the practice of dismantling a house and re-building it, or using the materials in another structure. Just this year, I walked into a shed in a Bonavista Bay outport and commented on how old it was. The owner looked at me surprised and told me it was practically brand new. I pointed to the clearly very old 10-inch-wide pine boards. Oh, he said, the wood. Well, that came from Billy Barnes's house, and before that Peter Barron's. The wood, in fact, was about 120 years old; the shed "new."

There is no justification for dumping garbage in the woods or heaving it over the side of a boat. But it has to be noted that traditional outport Newfoundland society did not have a lot of waste; therefore, there was no provision made for it. In the absence of that, there grew up a view of the backland as dumping ground; a mattress, car, or washing machine could find its way to the woods or over a cliff, simply because there was no other place, because it seemed the practical thing to do. Again, it must be remembered there was simply less waste before now.

To come back to the idea of the land as anything other than utilitarian, the woods and barrens did offer some recreation, for example trouting, but activities such as walking, hiking, and the pursuit of species to fill out a "life-list" were not part of the regular routines of most people,[4] perhaps because leisure itself was not a priority. And too, Newfoundland wasn't a setting that had historically inspired its settlers to poetry or painting. This is not to pass over the body of pre-Confederation literature and visual art we do have, but merely to state that artistic activity was not wide scale and was often the work of visitors. As for local response, most of our traditional ballads and songs have to do with people and their daily life and work rather than with an aesthetic appreciation of the land, or sea.[5]

What was regrettable in Newfoundland was the way the environmental movement came here. The quintessential formula for failure of a new initiative in an insecure or colonized society is to have outsiders come with missionary zeal to tell the natives they've got it all wrong. The purveyors of the environmental movement in Newfoundland came with, at best, little knowledge or understanding of the place; at worst, no respect for it. They brought the condescension of urban people to rural, of sophisticated to earthy, educated to uneducated, materially successful to economically disadvantaged. When I say "they," I don't refer to a specific body or organization, just the zealots sprinkled throughout the community. Our nomenclature was flawed: bullbirds are really dovekies, junipers are really larch, turrs are really murres. An incident unrelated to the environmental movement but instructional on this point might be cited here: Once, while in a shop in a small outport, I heard a hefty middle-aged man from mainland Canada ask a child of eight her name: Theresa Carey, she said shyly. Kerry? he boomed. There are no Kerrys in … Cove. How do you spell that? C-a-r-e-y, the timid response. Oh, *Carry*, Theresa *Carry*. The umbrella of this outsider's arrogance was wide indeed and included the presumption that he knew the "correct" way to pronounce the child's name.[6] This phenomenon—the dismissal and denigration of local knowledge and culture—has been a familiar part of life in Newfoundland; it perhaps reached its heights with the anti-sealing groups.

Consider an inshore fisherman who has a specialized set of skills and knowledge about the temperature and conditions of the sea, about wind, about fish habits and patterns, who eats what and when and why. All this is gained from his own observations combined with the knowledge of hundreds of years of the same kind of activity in the very same waters, passed on to him as patrimony. His resume, if such documents were relevant in his world, can never be equalled by any team of white-collar workers in Ottawa offices. There is no scientist working for the provincial or federal government who can match this knowledge. Fisheries bureaucrats talking about the inshore fishery in Newfoundland are as credible as a celibate priest pontificating about marriage.

Our flawed society has often been fertile ground for those who feel superior to us. We've never had the right kind of society where enough of our own go away, get educated, and come back. Instead, an individual and collective lack of confidence, aided by the encouragement of bad grammar and sloppy speech,[7] brought about a system where the articulate and better spoken were often from the outside. This fed beautifully (for those who wanted power) into a situation where many Newfoundlanders remained subservient and gave too much credence and respect to outsiders.

Nevertheless, the "environmentalists" coming here did meet with some resistance. For some of us, too, there was the complication of the tendency in the Newfoundland character toward fun-making, of rebelling against those who take themselves too seriously. The more earnest the messenger, the greater the motivation to take the mickey out of the message. So that in the early 1970s when I was a student, the green team met with no sympathy in me. Suddenly, having never thrown a chip bag on the ground in my life, I flagrantly littered whenever I felt I was being observed by zealous eyes. In an atmosphere of growing cultural and political nationalism, I—and others—asserted ourselves against the condescension and pedantry of outsiders. The French language signs then sprouting up on government wharves in Newfoundland at the time had the same effect on me: I was willing to stumble my way around Switzerland and France trying to sort out the challenges of the subjunctive, but I refused to speak French in "Canada." (Such reactions seem idle or naive in retrospect, but in the absence of a political channel for the passions and ideas flourishing at that time gestures were all we had.)

Countless Newfoundlanders have a cabin or cottage or tilt or shack or simply a spot—somewhere that represents for them a prized possession, or simply solitude. How many Newfoundlanders would say their hobby is some variation on going in the woods. And while these pleasures are priceless, they cost nothing. Enjoyment of them doesn't require expensive gear, gadgets, training courses, or fancy costumes. If you pass by the walking trails of Calgary or Banff, you will see an outdoor fashion show sponsored, you will think, by the designer Eddie Bauer. Experiencing the outdoors in many places, it appears, requires sleek, colourful clothing and matching this-and-that.

There is something refreshing about the other end of the spectrum, found often throughout this province. There's a pickup pulled over on the side of the road, and in the distance a lone trouter, scrappily dressed, hurries across the barrens trying to beat darkness; or a pair of berry-pickers with a single pot wanders out from the woods. Or the sight of an older couple in a meadow, bent over, stuffing a plastic supermarket bag with dandelion. These vignettes suggest a simplicity and sense of freedom hard to find elsewhere. The tidiness of Switzerland, the beaches of Spain lit up by a brilliant white sun, the endless landscape of Arizona, the Canadian Rockies, the cultivated fields of the American Midwest—I lived and walked through these as if they were movie props. Nothing seemed real: I couldn't connect.

The list of what Newfoundland does not have to offer is long and need not be entered here. What we do have is access to wilderness. We have a vast beautiful natural world with enough land, ponds, rivers, woods, beaches, coves, islands, berries, shrubs, paths, trails, and meadows for everyone. We should be able to live here and enjoy our land together, with a healthy collective respect and pride,[8] without restriction. We need a "revolution from within,"[9] not a set of rules or fines, to make it unacceptable to drive through a bog or wetland on a 400-pound "trike."

[1] The column, which first appeared in the St. John's *Evening Telegram*, is reprinted in my first book, *A View of Her Own* (St. John's: Long Beach Press, 1996), under the title "The new enemy of Newfoundland."

[2] Ray Fennelly, who walked across the interior of the island of Newfoundland, told me that when he found himself in the most "pristine" area, he looked down to see an empty Vienna sausage tin under his foot. His journey is recounted in *Canadian Geographic*, May/June 1992, Vol. 112, No. 3, pp. 38-49.

[3] *The Way It Was* (St. John's: Jesperson Press Ltd., 1990). See the chapter "Outport Recycling."

[4] Columnist and comic Mark Critch offers this Newfoundland perspective on certain forms of recreation: A mainlander asks, "Where would I find the best hiking trail?" The Newfoundlander replies, "No need to walk, b'y. I'll drive ya anywhere ya wants to go." See *The Express* (St. John's), July 12-18, 2000, Vol. 10, No. 7, p. 11.

[5] There are, of course, exceptions, the most obvious being the *Ode to Newfoundland.*

[6] A child's reaction to this kind of cultural confusion is beautifully described in the touching opening of Richard Rodriguez's memoir *Hunger of Memory* (Boston: David R. Godine, Publisher, Inc., 1982).

[7] I'm talking about grammar, not dialect. I refer to the vast number of high school graduates in the province whose basic grammar (for

example, subject-verb agreement) is so flawed they will never be able to compete successfully for certain jobs. The high incidence of this suggests institutionalized acceptance, which, it can be argued, is not all that far from tacit encouragement.

[8] The provincial government's push to privatize the outdoors—epitomized by the Tobin administration's handover of the majority of our provincial parks to private operators—works against the idea of collective ownership and will possibly have a negative impact on the environment. Changes in the fundamental nature of provincial parks can be seen, for example, at Northern Bay Sands where a large sign at the entrance advertises these park attractions: "9 pcs. Chicken, Fries & Gravy, 2L drink, $15.95."

[9] The title of Gloria Steinem's book about self-esteem (Boston: Little, Brown and Company, 1992).

First published as "Some Reflections on the Newfoundland Outdoors" in *From Red Ochre to Black Gold,* 2001

A Licensed Cup of Tea

ONCE UPON a time in a land far away, a harmless couple named Joe and Jane threw some gear in the back of the car and set off on their annual camping trip.

They drove an hour or so, found a place to leave the car, and walked a couple of miles in to one of their favourite ponds.

They'd just arrived at the pond and begun to set up the tent when Joe casually asked Jane if there'd been a lineup when she'd gone for the permit.

"I didn't go for the permit; you said you would," said Jane, and then ensued an argument in which each blamed the other for forgetting the government licence.

For one brief moment, they considered camping without it, but just as the temptation occurred to them, a helicopter flew overhead, swooped down slightly, and brought them back to their senses.

"Can't risk it," they agreed, and walked back to the car.

Back in the city, they lined up in the government offices.

Four hours later, they headed out the highway and made the long trek back into the woods.

Now Joe and Jane were tired. It was getting late and, as soon as the tent was up, Joe put the kettle on the fire for a second cup of tea.

"Ah," sighed Joe, "there's nothing like a cup of tea in the woods."

"True," said Jane. "Good thing you got Permit 8."

Joe looked confused, reached into his pocket, and hauled out a crumpled piece of paper.

"Permit A," he read. "See Permit B for Extended Boil-Up Coverage."

"Sure, they'll never find out," said Jane, and the temptation was just occurring to them when a helicopter flew overhead.

"Can't risk it," said Joe.

"No," said Jane, and off they went to find the car again.

Back in the city the office was closed, so they spent the first night of their summer holiday at home.

Early the next morning they drove to the Boil-Up Registration Building. The lineup was long, the forms extensive, but by 5 p.m. everything was in order. It was too late, though, to head to the woods, so they spent the second night of their vacation at home.

Back at the site at noon the next day, the tent was up, the kettle was boiled, and an afternoon of trouting lay ahead of them. Jane reached for her creel and fished out a dirty-looking crock of nice juicy worms.

"Where are you going with them?" asked Joe.

"Trouting," said Jane.

"Not with them," said Joe.

He took out a tiny ruler and measured the little things, one by one.

"No," said Joe. "Too big and juicy. You've got to use the government ones."

"Couldn't we risk it just this once?" asked Jane, and the temptation was just occurring to them when a helicopter flew overhead.

"Come on," said a wary Jane, and off they headed to the city to the new Government Worm Depot. Dutifully, they began to fill our their requisition form.

"They want some lot of information," said Jane.

"Yes," said Joe. "And how are we supposed to know how big the trout will be? And whether they'll be speckled or mud?"

But they persevered and off they went again.

"We've lost three days of our vacation," moaned Jane.

"Yes," said Joe, "but we're off now and there's nothing more the government can say about it."

And so it was that at about 6 p.m. on the third night of their vacation, Joe and Jane finally settled in. The tent was looking cozy, supper was finished, and just before his second cup of tea, John wandered off by himself.

"Where are you going?" asked Jane.

"I ... ah ... got to go to the woods," said Joe.

"Oh," said Jane

"Joe?" said Jane.

"What?" said Joe.

"Is that covered under Permit B?"

"I don't know," said Joe, and just as it was occurring to him to risk it, a helicopter roared overhead.

"Run, Joe, run," cried Jane, but her shouts were lost in the roar of the descending helicopter ...

Evening Telegram, March 4, 1990

Goodbye "Newfie"

IT'S TIME to take the word "Newfie," tow it out to sea, and sink it.

And while we're at it, let's load up a crate with all the Newfie paraphernalia and bury that, too. I mean "genuine 'Newfie' souvenirs" like mugs with handles on the inside. Where did that come from anyway? Is there a tradition here I don't know about of drinking tea like that? The folklore crowd has never mentioned it.

Whatever the Americans may have meant by it when they brought the term into prominence in the 1940s, the word "Newfie" has come to mean someone stunned, who talks funny and drinks too much. And it has grown from a word—perhaps a harmless one—to a cultural concept. Regrettably, it is Newfoundlanders who are busy packaging and selling it.

One of the most popular forms of entertainment that Newfoundlanders choose to provide for tourists is the screech-in. A man dressed in the traditional clothing of the fisherman stands before the audience. This is supposed to bring laughs. But it's the Newfoundlanders in the audience who start the laughter. After all, why would visitors laugh? There's nothing intrinsically funny about oilskins and sou'westers. Yachtsmen wear them with pride.

What a curious thing we've done, turning our traditional occupations and way of life into an object of scorn and mockery. Do the Swiss have Fondue Nights for Foreigners, where bankers in three-piece suits stand before the audience and everyone laughs?

It is the same disturbing impulse that makes Newfoundlanders tell Newfie jokes. Needless to say, there is nothing about the jokes that is peculiar to Newfoundland. They are the same unimaginative and trite put-downs that are told about every minority. What is unusual about Newfie jokes, however, is that they are acceptable. A Newfie joke is probably the only joke you could get away with telling on national radio. The argument for doing this rests largely on the fact that it is Newfoundlanders themselves who sell the joke and, in fact, the whole image.

It's a dangerous thing for us to be at, really, telling our visitors and our children that there is something basically stupid about us and that we're not to be taken seriously. Why do we do it?

It may be like the fat kid calling himself "fatty." If you say it yourself, it takes the sting out. There's an illusion that you're controlling the use of it and its meaning. You convince yourself that when others use the word, they do so as you would yourself.

Or perhaps another reason Newfoundlanders hang on to and promote the "Newfie" image has something to do with a genuine deep-seated desire to retain some sort of separateness from mainstream North America. We want to reassure ourselves that we are different—all that business about "another world next door"—and that we have our own culture. We do have our own culture: our ballads and folklore, our way of speaking, our humour, our maritime heritage, and the hardiness and heroism that were part of that. But the colonial mentality that lasted far too long here kept us from seeing validity in these things. When the label "Newfie" came along with its accompanying image, we grabbed it.

We have also confused an important part of our heritage—our tendency not to take ourselves too seriously—with the telling of Newfie jokes. But there is no connection between the kind of gentle humour recorded for us by Ted Russell and Art Scammell and the inanity of ethnic jokes, whether they concern a wop, a dago, or a newfie.

This confusion between Newfoundland humour and "Newfie" jokes has led to the unpleasant trap we find ourselves in when we protest "Newfie" jokes. Where's your sense of humour? we're asked. Don't take yourself so seriously, we're told. And, not wanting to seem unfriendly or act like spoilsports, we are pressured into participating in put-downs of ourselves. That somehow reassures us that we are indeed a happy province.

The other aspect of the trap is the fact that, because so many Newfoundlanders do propagate the "Newfie" word and image, protests against this practice are made impossible. However carefully you may try to educate the offender, you are met with the unarguable fact that the image is condoned and supported by Newfoundlanders.

When I'm told a "Newfie" joke, there's a look of genuine surprise on my face, much the same as there would be on the face of a black person who's just been told "I know tons of nigger jokes." My look of astonishment invariably brings the same response—"It was a 'Newfie' who told me." In other words I have no right to protest.

Trying to break out of this pattern is not easy. Any remark or activity in Newfoundland that would be considered nationalistic elsewhere brings forth the unpleasant labels here of jingoist, xenophobe, narrow. Yet other nations and peoples are permitted a degree of national pride. Are we somehow not valid as a people? I feel quite real myself.

The issue of the "Newfie" joke and the accompanying concept may not seem a serious one. But when you consider how it is used, the problems in our consciousness that it suggests, and the consequences of it, it becomes alarming. When you add the most curious dimension of all—that it is Newfoundlanders who are eagerly selling it—it becomes a cause for grave concern.

In a sophisticated country like Canada, the day will come when the word is no longer acceptable. We can wait until the anthropologists decide that it is inappropriate for us and teach us the importance of a wholesome self-concept—they may even find a new name for us. Or we can get rid of it now ourselves.

Evening Telegram, November 19, 1989

My Uncles Didn't Dance

ONE NIGHT, walking home from a choir rehearsal, I was going over in my head our conductor's new arrangement of the Newfoundland folksong "A Great Big Sea." She'd scored it for three-part female choir and piano. It's a catchy arrangement in a style welcome in classical choral repertoire. I thought again of the warring factions in the debate about Newfoundland music, the accusation that classical arrangements are an act of appropriation. I was still musing about this when I walked into my house, flopped on the couch, and flicked on the TV.

Here was Great Big Sea, the high-energy Newfoundland "trad" group who take their name from the well-known folksong. They play traditional music in a contemporary style using guitar, mandolin, concertina, accordion, bodhran, tin whistle, bouzouki, fiddle, and button accordion. The boys are compelling; when you start to watch, you can't walk away. The leader, Alan Doyle (alas, no relation), is a supremely gifted performer. He's not like those pop icons who look like they're on duty tour—glum dudes too cool to smile. The look on Doyle's face is unabashed ecstasy, and it's infectious.

The crowd was wild—new light on the sober citizens of Ottawa! The show was from the civic centre, part of the GBS national Road Rage tour. Here was the traditional Newfoundland ballad "Jack Hinks" transmogrified, Jack with a new hard drive.

It was like watching the Rolling Stones do "My Bonnie Lies Over the Ocean." The metre had been changed from its original 6/8, which gave the piece its gentle, rollicking sea shanty feel, to 2/4. The new metre and fast tempo drive the story of this "sea-faring, sail-making, gamboling, capering, grog-drinking hero—Jack Hinks." Syncopated bars disturb the metre to punch out certain lines: "we were bashed / on / the / rocks like hard / hunted / fox." In my head I could still hear Omar Blondahl and Alan Mills singing versions of this song, each of their recordings sounding like musical fireside chats—casual and chummy. I've sung it myself, too, hundreds of times but this was like no Jack Hinks I had ever heard.

In the middle there's a wild accordion "break" based on a traditional Newfoundland tune. Back to a hale and hearty Jack, in the full thrust of life, having had a near miss in a storm at sea. Another change in metre—a few measures of a waltz this time— to tell us he'd been saved "by Providence kind, who so eases the wind, and on sailors so constantly thinks." At the end, even listening to the recording without the benefit of visuals, it's as if you can see Jack step forward, put out his hand, and introduce himself with a nod and a wink. "Jack Hinks": the lead vocalist speaks rather than sings the last words, as is the way with many traditional singers. The piece concludes with a simple guitar chord. Jack's done.

That performance to my mind settled the debate of who's allowed to do what with "traditional" Newfoundland music.

Ah, Newfoundland music! I've spent my lifetime on both ends of this sticky spectrum. I have rolled around my living floor with tears in my eyes, laughing at the truly bizarre sounds emanating from mainland children's choirs singing "I'se the B'y." Yet I will go to my grave defending their right to take a folksong and do with it what they will. A folksong is up for grabs, but in Newfoundland there's a tight, snobbish circle who believe there is only one path of a folksong: it must be sung as it was traditionally sung. (There is little documentation to guide us here, however; it *is* an oral culture.) Preserving a piece of music as a museum piece or artifact is noble, and without that effort we might have lost our music, but when preservation moved into the territory of artistic tyranny, we arrived at a defining moment in the history of traditional Newfoundland music: *the great irony*. Purists holding fast to the notion that Newfoundland music belonged to the people removed the very democratic nature of it, laying out rules of who could sing a song, and how. The essence of the music was its accessibility: the music belonged to everyone. Songs were sung by the people, unaccompanied, or with the simple addition of a few instruments at hand, usually a fiddle or accordion. Ability to read music wasn't a factor as the songs were passed on orally. But when purists placed a defining stranglehold on the quintessential way to sing or perform a folksong, they did a cultural flip: they took ownership and made exclusions. An oboe player who knew his instrument was perfectly suited to a plaintive lament such as "She's Like the Swallow" was scoffed at: get out of here and stick to Haydn. There were no oboes in early Newfoundland! Determining that a school band sounded silly playing "The Sealer's Song" or that a choir singing "Petty Harbour Bait Skiff" in four-part harmony was laughable was contrary to the original spirit of traditional music. If you were a classically trained musician, you dared not approach Newfoundland music; if you did, you were spoiling it. The response of the musical bullies was a definite and territorial Paws Off!

Choirs the world over sing rhythmically and harmonically sophisticated arrangements of their country's folksongs, as well as new works of art created from those melodies. There is no exclusivity. Take Joseph Canteloube. Just as well he wasn't a Newfoundlander. Canteloube was born in the Auvergne area of France in 1879. When he was a young man, he roamed around the Auvergne, seeking out authentic singers and hearing them sing the songs of the region. He wrote down the songs with care and accuracy and later published four volumes of them. These are folksongs, nonsense songs, playful love songs, pastoral songs, songs of the cuckoo. Out of these songs he made an imaginative and rich cycle of nine pieces set for soprano and piano (or soprano and orchestra), his colourful *Songs of the Auvergne*. In Newfoundland, such an activity before recent years was anathema. Young Joseph would have been dragged up to Gibbet Hill for his villainy, he and his manuscript flung into Deadman's Pond.

Béla Bartók composed challenging string quartets but he also spent his lifetime collecting the songs of his native Hungary. Beethoven and Haydn arranged and set Scottish folksongs. Antonin Dvořák worked the native music of his country, Czechoslovakia, into his art; when he lived in the United States, it was some of the indigenous music of that country—"what are called the Negro melodies," he said—that caught his ear. It's not uncommon for composers to fill up their music with the melodies and rhythms of their country. But when a Newfoundland song is arranged as a classical piece, there's a rolling of the eyes, a shaking of the head, a pained and worried look that suggests *all is now lost*:

history, heritage, tradition, authenticity, gone—stolen by elitists.

But Newfoundland is a colony in recovery, and the desperate effort to retain our music in an authentic way is comprehensible to some extent. The new tyranny over folk music was part of a larger cultural despotism and was a by-product of the neo-nationalism that awoke in the 1960s and 1970s and centred around the notion that there was one "true" Newfoundland. There was a conception of this place fixed firmly in some minds that didn't allow for deviation, and it squeezed out much of the truth of our present as well as our past. Anything that fell outside the prescribed defining characteristics of "Newfoundland culture" was heresy. Newfoundland meant outport, it meant fishing, it meant poor fisherfolk; everything else was false. And here's the thing: this bullying assertion, this putting forward and giving value to all things outport, was a natural, understandable, and *probably necessary* corrective to the fact that the arts and Newfoundland culture had fallen into odd hands. It was difficult to find Newfoundlanders in positions of influence in what's broadly called the "cultural sector." Brits and Brit-wannabes—Newfoundlanders who'd never crossed the ocean but who had English accents—tended to fill positions in the arts, in the provincial arts and culture centres, in local amateur theatre, in groups dedicated to "the folk arts," at CBC Radio, even in the Faculty of Arts at Memorial University.

There's a tale told of a talented CBC television producer, a Newfoundlander, who turned to his colleagues one day and said, "Come on, boys, let's go down to Quidi Vidi [the closest cove to St. John's harbour] and go out in a boat so we can sail in through the Narrows"—an allusion to the belief that Newfoundlanders were often passed over for jobs and promotions in the cultural arena, in favour of those from away.

When I was a student at Memorial University in 1974, there was a plan that on March 31 (the 25th anniversary of the "feast of Confederation," as we mockingly called it), Newfoundlanders working in the areas that housed the humanities departments would go to work that day with their faces blackened with shoe polish, taking a page from John Howard Griffin's experiment described in *Black Like Me*. It was a fantasy because Newfoundland consciousness was not high enough for significant participation, and the plan was too hard to execute with so few conspirators. (A plot I was *not* part of was to blow up Pearson's Peak. Happily, the patriot in that case was visited by a heavy dose of good sense and he nixed the idea himself a few days before.) There were exceptions, but our scheme would have made a statement as the "white" professors from away and the "black" cleaners and administrative staff (Newfoundlanders) went about their business. Our motivation was a frustration born of sitting passively in front of professors who daily expressed contempt for us. After years of living and teaching in Newfoundland, some still refused to pronounce the name of the place as we did, holding on to some colonial version they'd learned before they came over. One Oxbridge professor, unable to accept where he'd ended up, regularly gave himself away; he said "here" when he spoke of England, "there" when he spoke of the new world.

This colonialism was the fertile breeding ground for young Newfoundlanders waking up to a Newfoundland consciousness or nationalism in the 1970s, a period described by Sandra Gwyn as a renaissance in Newfoundland art. The support, money, and performance opportunities for most music and theatre were under the control of a "director of cultural affairs," a position and title reminiscent of minor functionaries in Gilbert and Sullivan's *Titipu*. Around the real and symbolic figures of cultural power, there grew up indigenous theatre collectives like CODCO and The Mummers Troupe and the groundbreaking band Figgy Duff. Things happened quickly and soon there was a much-needed reversal in who "owned" Newfoundland culture, but there was one unfortunate piece of fallout: the baby that went out with the bathwater was classical music. Not native, not indigenous, it was dismissed as part of a culture that had been imposed on us and, in the minds of some, had nothing to do with us. It was shoved out from the canon of acceptable Newfoundland artistic activity. Perhaps it has something to do with a weird sense we have of ourselves: there is something laughable about singing our songs in a certain way, as if the songs—or perhaps we ourselves—are not worthy of such fanciness.

For my own part, I was in something of an unusual position. I was urban, and around that time in Newfoundland you could scarcely qualify as a Newfoundlander if you were from St. John's. There were narrow definitions about what a real Newfoundlander was; all of a sudden pedigrees from outports were sought and touted up. One university professor from a small community on a remote coast showed up at Memorial University speaking with a British accent. Within a year or two, the carefully nurtured affectation was dropped; he threw off his loafers and started teaching class in his rubber boots. Outport was in, and the more legitimate your claim to this heritage, the more of a *real* Newfoundlander you were.

My parents were both from small outports, but in my childhood we had no connection with their places of origin. My four grandparents had died before I was born. My mother's family had long moved from her birthplace, and her seven siblings had left Newfoundland. There was no one remaining on my father's side who retained a connection to his birthplace, not even my father, who died when I was three. So the outport in my childhood, despite my parents' background, was a remote concept. (My mother did take me around during the summers to see outport Newfoundland. She taught me to respect the life and work of a fishing community, forbidding the word "bayman," a derogatory term for an outharbourman, in our house.) I was surrounded in school by girls who went to their grandmother's for weekends, who went "around the bay" for the whole summer, who were part of huge extended families. Whenever I phoned a classmate to chat about school or homework, there was an aunt or uncle in the background, someone there for dinner, or there to mind them because their father was away or their mother was ill. It looked awfully rosy in there, through the collective window of my girlfriends' homes. I was from a family short on home life, for my brothers were always away at boarding school or in the seminary or married. I had no uncles who danced. My great-uncles, all dead, had been writers, folklorists, balladeers, publishers. I had to walk in shame during those delicate years, was scarcely a Newfoundlander at all in the Nazi-Newfie kingdom of the late 1960s and the 1970s.

Yet I was a dedicated Newfoundland nationalist, ready to walk in the parade that would lead us out of Confederation. I was the gofer for my brother Bill, carting gear around the island as he made his ironic film *Pure Silver*, celebrating the 25th anniversary of Newfoundland's entry into Confederation. I behaved suitably outrageously to actors who were imported from away to work in local theatre groups. (I was, however, extremely polite to Rick Salutin, a Toronto playwright who arrived around this time to assist local theatre collectives.) And I felt like an undercover agent, toiling by day for Joey Smallwood as a writer and researcher for his *Book of Newfoundland*, knowing, with the certainty and purity of youth, that my healthy clear-minded anti-confederate stance was the right one: Smallwood had screwed Newfoundland. I had ended up, that summer, working for him accidentally. He had called the university asking for suggestions for a recent grad who could do the work, and I was recommended. He was a good employer, he paid well, and there was no job I could have been happier with, but I was aware of the double nature of my life.

At that time Mr. Smallwood's "office" was the second floor of a private home on Forest Road in the east end of St. John's. He worked in the master bedroom and my space was an open area adjacent to the main door, so that I saw the few visitors who came and went. I had heard Mr. Smallwood's voice on the radio probably 20 times a day my whole life; his voice and image had dominated Newfoundland until his defeat in 1971-72. This remote demigod, this bogeyman of my childhood, was now a small, funny-looking man, casually dressed in slippers and a silk lounging jacket, working about 10 yards from me. I felt like Dorothy when the wizard came out from behind the curtain. We had daily "meetings." I didn't say a word, just scribbled in my notepad how many print inches I was to write about each subject in the biography section. It was *the* summer of anti-confederate sentiment among the young, because of the 25th anniversary, and here I was working with the enemy.

A greater irony was Joey's own position, for this "father of Confederation" was shunted aside during the celebratory year because his Liberal party was no longer in power. He was a Newfoundland patriot in his own way, attempting a monument to Newfoundland's past with his book. I was a daily witness to Joey burying himself in his work as the grand party went on around him. A loyal band of supporters tried to cobble together a small corner of it for him, a parallel celebration, but it was the poor man's feast. A dinner was planned for a school auditorium in Conception Bay. Around the office, it was assumed I would go. My whole summer was spent in the anti-confederate underground; now here I was expected to attend a dinner honouring this icon of Confederation! At that time, I lived in jeans and workboots, making exceptions for wakes and funerals. I drove to Bay Roberts and, in the parking lot of the school, squatting in my green Datsun hatchback, I struggled into a bra, skirt and blouse, nylons and dressy shoes, an impostor on many fronts as I walked into the school auditorium. I couldn't say no. Yes, he was former Premier J.R. Smallwood, he was the "only living father of Confederation," he was the focus of all my anger about Newfoundland's loss of nationhood—before I met him. Now, he was my tolerant employer, who treated me well, called me "Miss Doyle," and picked me up once when I was hitchhiking. He was also an old man, left out of the best party in town, a party celebrating the event he created. He was like a puzzled husband refused admittance to his own anniversary dinner. He had been a tough, fierce, ruthless politician, yet at some level he did not understand this turn of events. There was a naive streak in him—perhaps a romancing brought about by age. He was hurt.

This, then, was my day job that infamous summer. My night job was sitting in Bridgett's Pub, being cynical, ranting and roaring about Confederation, and sewing miniature Newfoundland flags (the Pink, White, and Green) on my knapsack. If we'd known about body piercing, we would have adorned ourselves with symbols of our "secret nation." I hung out with the actors my roommate, Maddy Williams, worked with as they toured the island with their "pageant," moved by the sight of the sealers left on the ice to die, startled by the young actor who knelt and bared her breasts ("She's some brazen." "She's from Tronto.") as Mary March, one of the last of the Beothuks, is said to have done to reveal her womanhood to her captors.

I was a patriot, a nationalist, but I was separated from the crowd by one thing: music. It was as if wanting to play Haydn trios was an act of treachery. In Britain, Fairport Convention and Steeleye Span were playing "traditional" music in a way that was not traditional. They took this music and did with it what they would. They incorporated the instruments, techniques, and style of rock and pop and contemporary folk. Now in Newfoundland suddenly it was acceptable, even cool—*fabulous*—to move away from the traditional. Drums and electric guitars and basses were allowed. Amplification was in, everything was in, *except* a classical treatment of Newfoundland music, and classical music itself.

Yet what is the difference between a folksong arranged for string quartet or choir or concert band, and the same song arranged for and played by a rock band? And here's where the argument for retaining music as it was sung falls apart for me, for what emerges is not a purist trying to preserve music as it was, but a cultural despot defining what is permitted, selecting and excluding. Granted, the musicians of Figgy Duff were clever and imaginative in their arrangements of Newfoundland music, while Toronto composer Howard Cable was not. But if those who were interested in traditional music had been open-minded, there would have been more forays into classical composition and arrangement, and this field would have grown. Instead, the door was shut. Classical music was shunted aside and its practitioners made to feel awkward and unwelcome at a time when traditional musicians, poets, painters, actors, and writers were coming into their own. Music had been taught in schools in Newfoundland more than drama or visual art or creative writing, and there had been many more choirs than drama clubs or visual arts classes. It is sad that in Newfoundland, where music is the art most enjoyed and practiced by most people, the art form that has lagged furthest behind is the composition and arrangement of classical music.

The Newfoundland songs I first heard and sang were from a collection published by my father. In the 1920s, he had begun to write down the songs he heard in his travels around outport Newfoundland. He was in trade—manufacturing cod liver oil, distributing patent medicines and household products—and visited his customers personally, going about by boat. He persuaded the Canadian, American, and British companies he represented to buy ads and, in 1927, published *Old-Time Songs and Poetry of Newfoundland.* As he gave out the books free, they ended up in most Newfoundland households. On one page there was a song, on the opposite page a picture of the product he was advertising. It was a brilliant idea of a man ahead of his time, and it was the work of a patriot. My father believed the story of a country was as likely to be found in its songs as in its formal records and documents. He prefaced his introduction with this epigraph: "Let me make the Songs of my Country and I care not who makes the Laws." (Later, in the 1950s, he suggested publicly that every child in Newfoundland spend part of the school day singing our songs; this would give them greater joy later in the music "of their country," and "add something worthwhile to their accomplishments.")

That first collection (and his 1940 and 1955 editions) was a rich mix of songs about disasters at sea, sealing, love won and love lost, the Newfoundland railway, and politics. One song came out of the 1869 election fought largely on the issue of confederation with Canada. "The 'Antis' of Plate Cove" was written by Mark Walker, the talented Bonavista Bay songwriter from Tickle Cove, a community not too far from Plate Cove.

> *And now to conclude this short ditty:*
> *I hope a good lesson we've taught*
> *And touters sent here from the city*
> *Have learned that Plate Cove can't be bought.*
> *Our fathers came here to get freedom*
> *Their sons will not barter away;*
> *Then hurray for the "Antis" of Plate Cove*
> *The "Athens" of Bonavist Bay.*

Sometimes the songs related an incident or described a "time" (soiree), such as the party—and even the cake—immortalized in this song:

There was glass-eyes, bull's-eyes and fresh butter,
Lampwicks and liniment too,
Pastry as hard as a shutter,
That a billy goat's jaw couldn't chew;
Tabacco [sic] and whiskers of crackies,
That would give you the fever and ache
You'd crack off from the knees if you happen to sneeze
After eating this Trinity Cake.

Most of these songs and ballads were a hair's breadth from disappearing in our precarious oral culture. The collection saved them and popularized them, moving the songs around an island where the population lived in isolated communities along the coast. Songs could have been well known in one area and unknown in another. Publishing them validated the music sung around the island at home, at work, at play.

These were the songs I grew up with. In our house, when I was very young, Newfoundland songs were played on piano and on piano accordion by a talented group of my father's friends and his cousins. Traditional dancing, the fiddle, the button accordion, and the kitchen party were not part of my tradition. No dancing uncles. My father came from a line of balladeers and writers. His mother's brothers included Maurice Devine (founding publisher of the newspaper *The Trade Review*) and P.K. Devine, whose work includes *Devine's Folk Lore of Newfoundland in Old Words, Phrases and Expressions* (1937). Another uncle, John Valentine Devine, wrote one of the best-known Newfoundland ballads, "The Badger Drive."

My father himself wrote songs and parodies, including "The Merchants," "A Noble Fleet of Sealers" (sung to the tune of "The Old Polina"), and, in the late 1940s, more than one anti-confederate ballad. "All Gone Now" blamed Confederation for the scarcity of rabbits on the Bonavista Peninsula in the early 1950s. He also wrote a parody of "The Cat Came Back." This tells the tale of the cat who survives many attempts on her life. In my father's version, the cat is taken on various Newfoundland adventures: she is dynamited, she is put on a train going west, she's dropped from a plane over Baccalieu Island, and she's sent to the ice (the seal hunt):

> Gave her to John Blackmore to take out to the ice
> And drown her in a bobbin'-hole, which wasn't very nice,
> But the crew they couldn't find her though they searched in all
> their bunks,
> For the cat she ran ashore one night and crawled upon
> the Funks.

And on it goes until:

> The cat lay by the radio and dreaming one fine day,
> When someone turned on CBC and it began to play;
> The cat she looked around a bit and then she raised her head,
> And when they played "O Canada," the cat dropped dead.

At the time that Newfoundland's nationhood was being voted on, and then voted out, my father was producing for general distribution professional recordings of Newfoundland songs. He hired a male vocal studio quartet in Toronto to make recordings, privately produced by RCA, of "Tickle Cove Pond," "The Sealer's Song," "The Hardy Sealers," "The Badger Drive," and "The Old Polina." He gave these out to customers and friends. They have almost completely disappeared. A few years ago, I got a phone call from a man who told me he was leaving Newfoundland for good—his children had settled out west. His house was on the market and he was holding a sale for much of his valuable pre-confederation Newfoundlandia. There was something he wanted me to have, if I would come by.

I went to the home of this stranger, feeling sick that the age-old need for work had not only driven his children from Newfoundland but this retired generation as well.

"Your father gave this to my father," he said, and passed me a homemade wooden box, a few inches bigger and thicker than a long-playing record. The back of the box was a solid piece of wood, the front consisted of four or five slats, as if ends of wood had been salvaged to make this case. The whole thing was held together by screws. On the box in blue ink was written: "Two Gramaphone [sic] Records of Nfld Songs. Given me by Gerald S. Doyle, 1948. To open, unscrew [arrows point to the left and right]."

The labour, the care, that had gone into the casing! This man's father had built a housing for the records, too precious to trust to a paper sleeve. I know of many beloved recordings, but I have never seen a box built to hold a record. I was moved, too, to think of the moment between the two men in this house, a few hundred yards from the Colonial Building, the seat of government, in the same year that the country of Newfoundland voted itself out of existence. On the morning of April 1, 1949, Newfoundlanders woke in their new country of Canada, but no one owned their souls. My father carried on with his own gestures and expressions of patriotism. The extraordinary recordings of the Commodore's Quartet were one small part of that. These close harmony arrangements sung by the musical and hearty voices of the Commodore's Quartet are as untraditional and as remote from Newfoundland as you can get—and they are my favourite arrangements of Newfoundland songs.

My father was unusual. He wasn't an academic, or a professional musician, or a folklorist coming from away to study us. He was a businessman, and he was at the very early days of collecting Newfoundland songs. I love the fact that the songbooks were tied up with the promotion of his business, but business wasn't cool in the 1970s when traditional music was on the rise in Newfoundland. Gerald S. Doyle and the songbooks were dismissed, not by the people but by a small crowd of the ascendancy in the traditional music scene. The criticism sometimes levelled against the songbook was that it was a collection of well-known songs. (This brings to mind Yogi Berra's comment about a certain club: no one goes there anymore because it's too crowded.)

In 1990, Newfoundland producer Kelly Russell asked some of our best musicians to choose a well-known Newfoundland song and record it as they liked. This CD, *Another Time*, opened up the possibilities of new treatments of familiar songs in a way that was acceptable to the musicians in the "trad" music scene. *Another Time* presents 12 traditional Newfoundland songs, mostly from the Doyle songbook, in non-traditional ways—blues, wonderful saxophone playing wandering around familiar melodies, Latin rhythms, a Caribbean flair to "Jack Was Every Inch a Sailor." There's even what I would call a chamber music scoring of "Tickle Cove Pond," with fiddle, guitar, cello, and a keyboard sounding something like a harp. Ron Hynes sings this sweet song with its quintessential moment in Newfoundland music, describing how and why a song might be written to preserve a story or incident. The song tells of a man coming home from the woods with a load of firewood in the spring of the year. On this particular day, Kit, his mare, warns him not to take the shortcut across the pond, the ice is too thin.

> *I knew that the ice became weaker each day,*
> *But still took the risk and kept hauling away,*
> *One evening in April, bound home with a load,*
> *The mare showed some halting against the ice road*
> *And knew more than I did, as matters turned out,*
> *And lucky for me had I joined in her doubt.*
> *She turned 'round her head, and with tears in her eyes,*
> *As if she were saying: "You're risking our lives."*
>
> *All this I ignored with a whip-handle blow,*
> *For man is too stupid dumb creatures to know*
> *The very next minute the pond gave a sigh,*
> *And down to our necks went poor Kitty and I.*

He called for help and two reliable families, the Oldfords and Whites, came along. Then the vignette that captures the songwriter on the spot:

When the bowline was fastened around the mare's breast
William White for a shanty song made a request.
There was no time for thinking, not time for delay.
So straight from his head came this song right away:

"Lay hold William Oldford, lay hold William White,
Lay hold of the hawser and pull all your might,
Lay hold of the bowline and pull all you can"
And with that we brought Kit out of Tickle Cove Pond.

Great Big Sea's "Jack Hinks" makes the argument that good musicians can take a traditional song and do with it what they will. So does Joseph Petric and Guy Few's recording of Newfoundland music arranged by Andrew Huggett. I don't believe in ownership or exclusivity. Jim Joyce has recorded "Hard, Hard Times," a straightforward but beautiful arrangement of perhaps our best ballad, with plaintive commentary from the harmonica. The same song was recorded by Ron Hynes and the Wonderful Grand Band, a powerful and moving, but entirely different, rendition of this great song. For every pebble on the beaches of Newfoundland, there's a professionally mastered recording, a homemade cassette, or simply someone singing somewhere. We're all at it. The field is wide and includes jazz, country, blues, bluegrass, composed songs—like Ron Hynes's "St. John's Waltz" and his "Atlantic Blue"—as well as classical arrangements such as D.F. Cook's challenging (to the singers, not to the audience) "Lukey's Boat," his tender "The Morning Dew," and Valerie Long's moving setting for female choir of "Drowsy Sleeper," a gem she found in the Greenleaf and Mansfield collection *Ballads and Sea Songs of Newfoundland.*

If I were walking through the casbah in Morocco I would recognize the sound of a Newfoundland accordion player, and don't tell me there hasn't been one there. I know for sure that Newfoundland repertoire was once played for hours on a blazing hot afternoon in Crete on a sweet-sounding concertina purchased in Athens. The lonely musician and her friend entertained themselves to ward off death by heat exhaustion, as buses to everywhere except their destination regularly passed by. (I've since purchased a dictionary with the Greek alphabet; next time I want the bus to Iraklion, I'll recognize Ιπάκλίον.)

Newfoundlanders are lucky: we are a people with a huge repository of music rich in stories, characters, and humour; songs of nostalgia, of loss, of the fearsome sea, of the beauty of the land. It's an integral and unifying part of us. Music gathers the Newfoundland diaspora when Buddy Wasisname and the Other Fellers and other talented groups criss-cross the country. Tens of thousands of people come out to see them, and sing with them. On the CD *100% Pure*, the audience (Ottawa again!) joins in for "Song for Newfoundland." There is no dispute here, musical or otherwise, in the spontaneous singing by the unofficial choir, that lonesome band of exiles:

> *She's a rocky isle in the ocean,*
> *She's pounded by wind and by sea,*
> *You may think that she's rugged and cold,*
> *But she's home sweet home to me.*

Queen's Quarterly, Summer 2004

As Irish as a Song

MY NAME is Doyle. I hang off a tree with Devines, Foleys, Coffeys, Sullivans. I can sing and play 132 Irish songs. You might think me Irish.

In my childhood, St. Patrick's Day was a holiday. Colourful banners and flags streamed from the Basilica high on a St. John's hill across the street to the Benevolent Irish Society below. At home, we raised an Irish flag and sang the ballads of Thomas Moore. Our speech converted "I've told her" to "I'm after telling her." We said "ye" for you, and "minding youngsters" for babysitting children. Our sentences were sprinkled with "poor soul" and "God rest his soul." If we saw a hearse in front of the church on a sunny day, we'd cheerfully mutter, "Happy is the corpse that the sun shines on." We walked to school bundled in drab woollen coats and kept a bandana handy in case we needed to slip into the church. We were miniature Irish crones.

When I visited the mainland as a child, grownups would add up my red hair, fair complexion, and Newfoundland accent, and declare, she's so *Irish*. I would give a girlish smile of compliance, charmed to be thought so charming. When I stumbled into the writing of Edna O'Brien and Brendan Behan, I thought: That's *my* literature.

And yet I wouldn't know a caubeen from a cruishkeen. My connection to the old sod is remote. I'm a seventh-generation

Newfoundlander. Irishness flowed into my childhood in a reliable cultural conduit: music. It flowed like an intravenous drip from Blarney Castle to our convent school.

The Presentation Sisters arrived from Ireland in 1833. Young girls were still coming out to become nuns as late as 1911. One of the last of these—she'd left Tralee in the 1880s—was still giving piano lessons in the convent parlour during my childhood. On her 100th birthday she was carried out to the school and down the narrow staircase to the auditorium. She was eased into a humble throne, an armchair, and we sang for her "The Rose of Tralee" and "Bendemeer's Stream"—sang as if we ourselves had been raised in the streets of Tipperary.

We were wriggling through childhood under a heavy Irish shroud, but we never heard the word Ireland. I squint through the endless corridors of childhood memory; I squeeze my body tight trying to recall a reference. I block sound, trying to hear what Mother Aloysius is saying to the class, reading her lips, but Ireland is not there. Was there a single Irish story in all our readers? From school, I recall sleepy talk of Canada—reciprocity and car manufacturing. I remember a book with colourful child-heroes from many countries, but I can't picture an Irish colleen, poet or patriot. The curriculum was barren of Ireland. But the music was not, and the lyrics of a song can carry sentiment, fictions, and fact.

Oh Paddy dear and did you hear the news that's going 'round,
the shamrock is forbid by law to grow on Irish ground;
St. Patrick's Day no more we'll keep, his colour can't be seen,
for there's a bloody law against the wearing of the green.

I know the story, but not from scholarly research.

Some years ago I was in the home of an 86-year-old man a few days before he died. He startled his children by sputtering out a song they'd never heard before, as if a tightly locked memory had loosened a little, unfolding a ballad of cowards, patriots, and a freed land. That's one way to pass on the story of Wolfe Tone, and the Rebellion of 1798.

When I meet second-generation Canadians, I'm often startled by how remote they seem from their parents' home countries. In one generation—20 years, say—the links have weakened, grown rusty, as families hug tight to their new country. The power of music! My people were gone from Irish soil 150 years before my childhood, but Ireland was the world we brushed up against through the closeted nuns—that was the country we travelled to in their songs.

We were growing up in Canada (well, Newfoundland) in the 1960s. Across the country, youngsters our age were cheerfully counting "one little, two little, three Canadians" as Bobby Gimby lured crowds to Expo '67. We were mourning the boy-hero Kevin Barry, who "high upon the gallows tree" hanged "for the cause of liberty." As Canadians sang happy birthday to their 100-year-old country, we squeezed onto choral risers, praised the 18th-century patriot Napper Tandy and shared dreams and promises of a "return" to Galway Bay with an ancient Irish nun.

National Post, March 17, 2006

Parents: Get Thy Children to a Clarinet

I'M NOT a professional athlete. I've never been asked to endorse a pair of sneakers, but I have played some serious ball. When the photos were developed, it did seem shameful—me cutting a rough swath up and down the field, trampling, tackling, and squatting people who were, well, to be honest, five and six years old. Still, if I'd played with people my own size, it would hardly be fair—to me.

I was turned out of gym the first day of high school. I was holding a badminton racket as if it were a ukulele. Mrs. B. sealed my fate with eight words: "You can't be as stupid as you look." I slunk out and hid in a corner of the music department for the next three years, occasionally sending in forged excuses from Mother: "two months for the appendectomy scar to heal over," "persistent wheeziness," and "appears now to be contagious ..."

The result of this self-exile was that the heady feeling of shouting and scoring, the sweaty rush that buoys athletes came to me late in life, and only once—that day when restless grandchildren were desperate for a playmate.

Where was I in the intervening years? Lost down the end of a flute bore or standing on a choral riser. I missed out on sports but stumbled into life's greatest hobby—the one with the long shelf life and most rewards: music. And now I want to go door to door peddling music, persuading parents of its worth. Because once music took over my days, it shoved aside the curses of childhood: idleness and boredom.

Something's gotta grab you in those years when your appetites are large; something has to absorb the energy, satisfy the passion. Something that leaves no time to linger around corner stores or shopping malls.

Ah *but*, skeptical parents will say, peer pressure rules children. I argued for years, not me, I was never influenced by my peers, until I realized one day I had been a slave to peer pressure, but the crowd I wanted to be "in" with weren't the jocks or the cheerleaders, or even the beautiful people. My peers were fellow musicians.

Cool is defined by kids themselves—it's about what's cool to them. We may have looked like a crowd of nerds filing into the orchestra room, or dorks boarding the bus for music camp, but for us it was the jocks who were suspect, off in their exhausting worlds running mad around vast fields. Once we fell into music, that's where cool was. We wanted to get the good solos, compete in festivals, and play, play, play. Music seduced us, and *we were never bored.*

I missed out on sports because I was clumsy and self-conscious. I believed I was pathetic in that department, and probably was. I could do something about this now. I could call round to the girls I went to school with, rent a gym, buy a basketball and a whistle maybe, but what would we do? Stand in a gym and stare at each other? I was in a gym once. I was working at a summer music camp. There was a game between staff and kids. I stood in the middle of the court frozen with fear and when I saw that flying package heading my way, I ducked my front end so low that my back end rose. The ball bounced off my—well, let's just say I was the butt of that joke.

You can become athletic later in life by joining aerobics, or you can slide into gentler sports like golf. It's harder to take up music. Like any language, it's best learned young and it can travel with you down a long road. I sing in a choir with men and women from 21 to 75 years old. Music transcends age.

One of my resolutions this year is to spend half an hour a day at the piano. I am slogging through the scores of my favourite operas. My brain is getting a workout; so are my fingers and wrists. My memory's improving, and I'm getting to know the melodies better. It's good for my back, good for my shoulders. I walk away from the exercise refreshed, energized, and—you know those endorphins runners talk about? I swear they're coming out of my keyboard. I walk away high.

I still have a nagging feeling that I've missed out, and "agile" and "athletic" are words that won't turn up in my obituary, but when an opportunity appears, I intrude myself into the sports arena. Last fall, I was trudging along a path that borders a fenced ballpark. Something startled me in the bushes—a partridge, I thought, until a frustrated guy ran up shouting at me from inside the fence. I retrieved the ball and, with the force of 40 years of unreleased pitches, this incipient athlete, this wannabe ballplayer zealously fired into the air. I watched, amazed, as that small round parcel made it over the fence and settled into the guy's mitt.

I carried on walking, all warmed up with a new sense of myself. I was, of course, on my way to choir.

Globe and Mail, April 19, 2006

A Chorus Girl at Home: Sing, and Louder Sing

An aged man is but a paltry thing,
A tattered coat upon a stick, unless
Soul clap its hands and sing, and louder sing
For every tatter in its mortal dress …
                                    —W.B. Yeats

I AM late for the Christmas gig at the Home. I'm never in a hurry to cross into that country. My feet drag the last hundred yards up the driveway. It's cold but I dawdle, filling my lungs with a supply of clean air. Inside, I gag down the urge to retreat. I hear the choir warming up down the hall and remember why we are here. I throw my coat on a chair at reception and spread an old newspaper under my dripping boots. Soggy lines stare up at me: "ensuite with master, powder room on main, whirlpool and sauna, view." I head down the hall. The air is hot and oppressive, as if by some olfactory Orwellian trick the walls have been programmed to give off boiled cabbage. I catch up with the choir and file into the auditorium.

We are spared for most of the show, our eyes zoned in on the conductor, our inner eyes squinting to "see" the memorized words and notes. Between each set of songs there is a singalong; now, the conductor at the keyboard, our eyes are free to roam over the singing audience.

Old lips moving, but barely, as snatches of carols come back to them, chests rising and falling in unnaturally short breaths, chopping the long musical phrases we pride ourselves on. Some look as if they might expire in the effort to keep up as the song whizzes by, trying to gather them in. The sleigh is safely home and the passengers content again when I hear a lone rasped "Jingle" come from the front row, but the singer stops herself shyly when she realizes we're all done.

This is not a darkened theatre with unseen patrons. The institutional lighting is unforgiving. I am squeamish and want to turn away. What age does! How it robs and steals as it creeps along our bodies, knocking out power lines: power to walk, to see, to hear. It comes like an electrical storm with its claps of thunder, remote at first, distant warnings of the strikes to follow, filling us with fear as we strain to tell if it's approaching or moving off. An attack, one part of the body now in jeopardy, then a reprieve— until the next storm.

I shouldn't avert my eyes, I should look straight out into this community which I will not escape. I think of songwriter Eric Bogle's wounded soldier Willie McBride (in "The Green Fields of France") carried off the ship on his return to Australia: on the pier the crowd is waiting to receive the blind, the lame. Here are those wounded less dramatically, their skills eroded over time, eyes and ears failing slowly, mobility curtailed. Still, a leg gone is a leg gone. My eyes keep coming back to this one woman. She smiles as she sings, and the smile chips away at my memory.

"*Venite adoremus, venite adoremus, venite adoremus Dominum,*" audience and choir together sing. Perhaps it is the Latin that links me to childhood and brings into focus the younger face hidden inside the new old one. The smile has pushed away her wrinkles and muddy makeup and restored a woman I saw every morning of my childhood at the neighbouring church. Then it is as if this one recognition clears my vision and unmasks the others. Familiar features now appear through the crumpled folds and skin. Yes, that is Mr. ——, the slightly stooped man who dressed 365 days of the year in a black peaked cap, white silk scarf, and navy wool coat. He was a grown-up altar boy, willing to stand in when the boys failed to show. We'd laugh—the sight of him up there in street clothes, chasing after the priest, ringing the bell. These identifications are coming slowly, aided by clues like a gesture or a smile, as if their personalities have outlasted their housing. Those who sit impassive remain mysteries. And now as we sing the chorus of "Angels We Have Heard on High," a man in the front row suddenly perks up and joins us. *Gloooooooooooria in excelsis Deo.* He doesn't look old; some private infirmity has placed him here. It is the change in expression on his face that twigs me: he was a teacher both feared and mocked. These days I read his letters to the editor on social justice, peace, clean water. I will speak to him later to tell him I like his views.

I will? Am I so ageist and egotistical that I think he will be cheered by my approval?

The songs are sentimental. We've been singing "Merry Christmas Past" but the merry seems ironic. And now it starts. The well-shored-up self, the one who believed herself prepared for this starts to give way—the lyrics of the song, the faces, the apparatus of suffering are edging in on my resolve to get through this. Don't look. I'm melting. I'm at exactly that moment in life where old age stops being a concept and becomes the place where everyone is—Old Age lumbering toward me, every year more familiar faces in his cart.

It's stuffy here. Open the window, one of the sopranos mouths. More, others indicate with brisk nods, and the tall, slim alto, standing near the high window, reaches up again. We will all pass out, the whole choir will pass out. We're on this road together, the road of ancient parents with all the moral, human, even financial issues, the decision making, the transfer of power, of natural order, of who's taking care of whom. We're all on the path, those of us with parents here, and those farther back in the line but on their inevitable way.

"*I remember Christmas past,*" we sing, "*'round the Christmas tree. Funny how those mem'ries last, they come back to me.*" Lines that were too sentimental in rehearsal are now too tough to sing, lines about "*when we all believed.*" Suddenly the song is too much—for it is less about the joy of Christmas than it is about the memory, as if Christmas exists only in anticipation, and in the past. The song snatches even children's happiness and turns it into retrospective pleasure.

> *Never can return somehow, mem'ries have to do,*
> *Younger hearts are learning now Christmas joys we knew;*
> *All the little children seem to grow so fast,*
> *But, come December, they'll remember Merry Christmas past.*

We are fated, all of us, to be servants of memory.

Christmas: mad traffic, lineups, excess of food, too much drink. Families mingle, divide, divorce, and throw new faces into the mix. Christmas when hostilities and bitterness are stuffed under the surface long enough to get through the turkey; by the time the pudding is lit, tempers, too, are flaming. Christmas, with its evaporating expectations, its residual emptiness. Christmas, when a year's worth of family life is squeezed into short harried days, the family dynamic exercised rigorously.

The December litany intoned by the socialite:

"Twenty coming for Christmas dinner. Twenty!"

"Three parties in one night, I said to Ned …"

"Haven't got time to wipe me arse."

"Busy …"

"….. busy ………………"

"…………… busy ……………"

"…………………………. busy."

Time chased, pursued. Time parcelling himself out in small packages, stingy Time, always shortchanging us and leaving us wanting more, until we arrive at this last stop. Here, where time moves in, settles down, and mocks us. Here, where a sign on the bulletin board last week announced that the choir would come.

"Tomorrow?"

"Not tomorrow, Cissy."

"The next day?"

"No, my love, not this week."

"When?"

"Next week. Thursday, the 19th."

"Not tomorrow, nurse?"

"No, Cissy, not tomorrow. The choir comes next week."

Cissy scuffs back to her room in baby steps to begin the familiar eternity between breakfast and lunch.

We are singing "I heard the bells on Christmas Day, their old familiar carols play" when I am startled by another face, a man my own age, who must be here visiting. We used to be related. I stood around a piano and sang with his family for 10 Christmases; I remember their traditions better than my own. The Sunday between Christmas and New Year's reserved for the elderly maiden aunt and bachelor uncle who hosted the biggest feast of the year working for days, like the driven Babette in the film *Babette's Feast*, to produce their secret dishes. And now, instead of holding the alto line, my concentration is slipping—I'm falling somewhere I don't want to go. They are no longer mine. I am the enemy, the one who left. Focus. Think. Add a new harmony. The breadcrumbs on the tomato soufflé were the thing.

"Can I get you some more, Marj? You seem to like the 'cazzerole' best this year. I know you didn't like the trifle last year, so I sweetened it—the one with the chocolate on top, that's yours."

Get up from there now; if not, you won't make it through.

Where are we? My neighbouring alto saves me.

Four pieces left, I tell her. Four times three minutes a piece. That gives us 12 minutes more to not look, not think, not feel.

Some have come in mobile beds and specialized chairs. One elderly woman near the front is sitting up in a complicated chair-bed. A younger woman sits beside her, puts her face so close to the old woman's cheeks they must be touching. She looks like she is whispering, but she is singing directly into the old lady's ear, pulling back every few seconds, watching for a response. Forward, singing into the ancient ear, back to observe, forward, back, she is creating a rhythm of her own. There is such love in the gesture, such joy in the younger woman's face when she sees a glimmer in the old eyes. I am singing to them now, they are my private audience until I'm distracted: two rows ahead an old man is trying to clap along with a song but his hands never quite meet.

Across the sea of white hair, with patches of blue and patches of bald, I see a man in his 40s sitting with one arm around a frail elderly lady. With his free hand he holds a drink with a straw, offering her small sips. And now a trim, energetic woman steps up in front of the choir and begins to dance. Her rhythm is exact; she is precise in her movements as if she's just arrived from aerobics class. Another woman, less lucky in old age, begins to wave her hands, making large loose gestures like an unruly sign of the cross. Suddenly we realize she is conducting us, mirroring our director.

And in this room of the aged, the bare aged, perhaps there is relief at the release from girdles, buttoned shirts and ties; loose ankle socks welcomed, maybe, where tight stockings used to be. Here, we are beyond the campaigns to persuade us into believing we can purchase mortality with jars of creams and pills. No one torments the elderly, who have less buying power than their teenaged grandchildren. This crowd is left alone.

I swear off every year. I will not go back and do this and yet somehow we know collectively it is the most important thing we do. Later we will tell each other which song beat us down.

"'I'll be home for Christmas,' that's the one that gets me," says one of the sopranos.

"White Christmas," says another. "We had that Bing Crosby album—"

It's the only bit of music they get, we tell each other.

"Still, next year," one woman brings us up short, "I'm not

wearing glasses. I'll come, and I'll sing, but I don't want to see anything." She's still recovering not so much from her father's death here, as from his last years.

I need to share my news, but can't seem to say it: soon, I'll be buying the black marker to label my mother's clothes.

We wrap up: "We Wish You a Merry Christmas." I'm hurrying—aiming for the end of the corridor which will lead me fast into the pure night air. They're in their doorways, willing us to stop, as if they've waited all day for someone to come by, someone with time. At one doorway a well-dressed man in his 60s gives a small kiss to a frail crone. She looks at him, willing him to stay.

He glances at his watch.

"I gotta go, Mother. I'll be in Christmas Eve." He waits for some release.

She reaches for the sleeve of his jacket and tugs him back.

"Don't grow old, Paddy, my son. Don't grow old."

I look at the guy, wondering if he got it, the love she'd just thrown.

Up ahead, four rooms away, a tiny woman with tight blue curls is eyeing me. Even from here I can see her keen expression.

What excuse will be good enough to say no to this woman who, on the day I was born, was as old as I am now? What lie to convince her that five minutes of my time is too much to give, to her for whom a week, a day, an hour are equal in the new math of the aged where numbers don't matter much.

And as I walk the corridors, I am a child again, tagging along with my mother as we made the Christmas rounds, delivering gifts of stationery, chocolates, and smelly soaps. The last stop was here, at the Home. I had the child's horror of hard sights:

the legless man who travelled the corridors on a low wooden platform on wheels, the woman whose tongue flapped in and out of her mouth as steady as the wheels of a locomotive, the only strength left to her lodged in involuntary muscles. If we were lucky, Miss T. would come out to the small visitors' room at the reception. If not, we'd have to penetrate the Home farther, down those corridors, avoiding eye contact with the lonely, refusing to hear their hellos, shrugging off their attempts to reach out and touch. I was cross-eyed from looking first this way, then that, refusing to admit the images creeping into my peripheral vision. After the old woman's degeneration, worse again: up the elevator to the sick floor.

She was tall, thin, had a full head of dark curly hair and sat erect in her wheelchair. She was soft-spoken and had a tender smile never returned by me, the frozen kid counting the seconds to get out of there. Her hands were gnarled, as if they'd been clenched in anger when the wind changed. On the top of the bureau was a black typewriter, and I would paste my eyes on it, focusing on the word Remington.

On the way out, my mother would always make the same remark.

"How she gets those fingers around that keyboard, I don't know. It must take the whole day to type a few lines." But I paid no attention and only years later found in our bookcase a slim orange volume: *Autumn in King's Cove and Other Poems* by Bertille Tobin. I remember one line: *Our brief life here is only night, at close of which will dawn a day with human weakness passed away.*

Now, ahead of me, the exit door comes in sight, promising my life back. A minute later I'm putting on my coat and boots when I hear music from a nearby doorway. I peek in and see an old woman. She's alone in a far corner of the TV room, hunched over a piano, trying to marshal the necessary forces. The crumpled right hand tries to widen itself to make the reach, inching its fingers apart as if each one is pushing Sisyphus' stone. The unruly left hand refuses to be reined in; it hovers over the keyboard like a hunting fish-hawk then drops with a weak crash. Unwanted sharps and flats wander in. Eventually the sounds unscramble and a melody pokes through the cluttered notes. There is a book of carols propped up in front of her, but her eyes are focused far beyond this room. She is playing "by heart," "from memory," and the phrases take on new meaning.

I listen, sly audience of one. The carols carry us on separate secret journeys, wordless travels. In time, I steal away, lifting my booted feet to exit silently.

Reels, Rock and Rosaries: Confessions of a
Newfoundland Musician, 2005

A Chorus Girl Away

MUSIC IS a hobby that travels.

My first stage appearance outside my native land took place at Mount Allison University in Sackville, New Brunswick. Because I was raised in a household in which we still thought of Newfoundland as a country, I considered this my Canadian debut. I would like to say I'd been invited there or that I was on tour. In fact, it was Fun Night at a summer music camp. All the other "acts" were non-nation specific; the kids performing together weren't from the same place and didn't feel they had to make a statement. They mostly performed skits and campfire songs. But there is something about Newfoundlanders, as if there exists inside us a system of invisible magnets that exerts a pull when we come within a certain radius of one another, as if we're all hooked up to some version of a fish-finder.

There we were at Mount A and it was as if a siren heard only by Newfoundlanders had been activated and presto! we were in one place at one time, with an unstated notion that there should be official representation from our country. Standing among us kids was a huge man dressed in black pants and white T-shirt, a pleasant fellow with a booming voice who had a friendly teasing manner with the boys. The boys introduced him as "Br" (pronounced burr), the universal form of address used by Catholic boys for the Christian Brothers who taught them. He was on campus taking summer school and, yes, he knew how to dance. He was easily 6 feet tall and 250 pounds, but relatively light on his feet. At least he knew the steps. From that moment until the great night, we rehearsed in every spare moment until we got the "Lancers" (a popular Newfoundland quadrille) down. In my memory I try to convince myself that I ended up the piano player (the tune was "I'se the B'y"); I was a self-conscious, clumsy kid and would have entered any pact to spare myself going on stage *dancing*. We girls wore bright red skirts and white blouses, the boys wore white shirts and grey pants. I marvel at this now. Parents today could only wish for kids so innocent that they go off to a co-ed camp—a big deal for us because we went to separate schools—and, rather than drink, smoke dope, or screw one another, they get up on the stage in matching outfits and do the bloody Lancers!

The idea of carrying my patriotism abroad seemed natural and a few years later I found myself, solo this time, performing the "Ode to Newfoundland" on my knees in my university cafeteria.

When I had arrived on campus the first day at Mount St. Vincent University in Halifax, I knew no one. I was by myself in the frosh registration line. When it came time to have my photo ID made, I was asked my name. Then:

"Middle name?"

My middle name was Marie but when I opened my mouth, "Joseph" came out.

(It was like an unwanted visitation from Mr. Bean.)

"Your middle name is Joseph?" How is it that all those sucky seniors who end up "working" registration seem as if they're auditioning for jobs with the gestapo? They have that air of condescension exuded by women who work in high-end dress shops when someone other than a perfect size eight comes in.

"Yes." I was definite. (My confirmation name *is* Joseph. I had wanted to honour the Holy Family but the priest said I already had "Marie," which was really Mary, and I could hardly take Himself.)

So moments later, although I did not yet know what use I could make of it, I had an official university photo ID card with the name Marjorie Joseph Doyle. It seemed a good thing to have.

Later during that first semester, in the university cafeteria one day stories were going around the table, and I threw out, casually:

"In Newfoundland, every baby born after Confederation is named after Joey Smallwood."

There were a few guffaws but I could lie. My brother and I had perfected the art of lying in childhood on a need-to-lie basis involving, say, cigarette smoking or broken windows. I created a few good stories to back up my claim.

"You're kidding," said the gullible.

"I don't believe you. That's ridiculous," said the sophisticate from Montreal who'd been banished to an all-girls, nun-run university by her parents, who thought that removing the distraction of boys would help focus her grades.

I pulled out my student ID, as impressive a document as any of us had at that age and there I was: Marjorie Joseph Doyle. In the silence, with even the skeptic caught off guard, I forged on, letting myself be guided by Gilbert and Sullivan's Lord High Executioner of Titipu, adding "corroborative detail … to give artistic verisimilitude to an otherwise bald and unconvincing narrative."

"Well, I never really do this, but once a day we're supposed to face Newfoundland, kneel and sing a verse of the 'Ode.'" And down I went, singing the first line or two before one of the gestapo came charging toward me. Probably thought I was on mescaline when, in truth, I was locked into a childish sense of fun, left over from a girlhood in a convent school.

The ability of people to believe anything about Newfoundland because of their ignorance of it offers unlimited opportunities. It reached its heights for me later in Macomb, Illinois, after a music theory classmate at Western Illinois University learned I was from Newfoundland. "Wow," he said. "Your English is fantastic."

"Thank you," I said.

"So, what's your first language, anyhows?" He talked like Howdy-Doody.

"Latin." It sort of was: I spent so much time in church that "*Et cum spiritu tu tuo*" rolled off my tongue as easily as eeny-meeny-miny-moe and made about as much sense.

"Jeeze, I didn't think they still *spoke* Latin anywheres. Is it, like, the official language?"

"Sort of. There are so many Catholics there and they spend so much time in church, it just turned into the vernacular—accidentally."

"Wow."

But mostly when I played or sang away from home, it was not Newfoundland music. In Illinois, I played alto sax in a stage band and sang with the university choir in Arthur Honegger's *Le Roi David* (King David). In Madison at the University of Wisconsin, I sang Bach's oratorio *St. Matthew Passion*, a performance so long we had a supper break during it. In Barcelona, I sang with the *Orfeó Català de Barcelona*, the house choir of the *Palau de Musica*, pride of the Catalans, the repressed people of Generalissimo Franco. They'd been forced to suppress their language and culture during his long *dictadura*. The regime ended with his death in 1975; 10 years later, around the time I arrived, the Catalans were basking in their language and culture. I felt at home there, aligned with them in some inexplicable way, and comfortable because the Catalans and the Spanish are warm and easy people. When I reflect on my two years in Barcelona, I think I was *saved* by singing in the choir.

We rehearsed two nights a week, late, as the Spanish eat late. Our rehearsals began at 9 p.m. and ended at 11:30. Afterwards, I walked to a nearby square where taxis hung out. The uneasiness I felt walking in the downtown late at night, the cab rides, and entering the empty apartment at midnight—my mate worked late—were incidental, next to the joy of singing.

Language wasn't a problem. Choristers are used to singing in languages other than their own. The director, one of the myriad expatriate Brits living in Spain, conducted the rehearsals in his fledgling Catalan. He spoke in slow, simple sentences with a pronunciation mystifying for the native speaker, but perfect for the foreigner; with a smattering of French, Latin, and the Spanish I was starting to learn, I could get his drift. Besides, a good conductor communicates about phrasing or articulation as much by gesture or example as by explanation. There was always the fear I'd miss an announcement of a performance or a change in dress code, but in those cases someone would lean over and whisper to me in slow, careful Spanish.

We sang in Catalan once only, at a Christmas concert. We had finished our programme of standard repertoire and I was expecting to leave the stage when the choir began singing music unfamiliar to me. These were well-known Catalan carols such as "El Noi de la Mare" (these days I seem to hear this pretty carol everywhere). The music had not been passed out, or practiced, or mentioned. The conductor simply led the choir into an annual tradition. I stood mute in the middle of 80 people; I couldn't even "mouth the words" as the proud Catalans sang. We also sang in English once, when we sang Mendelssohn's *Elijah*. It was odd to be sitting in a rehearsal being drilled on your own language, but I didn't dare walk out, because the coach was a Brit who probably thought my English was unacceptable anyway.

We hit the road a couple of times a year. Once, we travelled to Aosta in the Italian Alps just before Christmas. We flew to Geneva and then bused our way up the snowy mountain into the cool dry air, driving from late afternoon with its fading winter light, to darkness. There was time before the performance to stroll the streets of this quiet Alpine town. We walked in bunches, a string of six or seven of us filling up streets that seemed to have no cars. Snow was falling, not sideways as it does in Newfoundland, carried on a harsh wind, but straight and regulated as if above us a theatre technician roamed a catwalk controlling the flow of snow: the rhythm was steady, the flakes consistent, and newly arrived snow remained white. It was a village of tiny shops. The storefronts were not the sweeping windows of the city with life-sized mannequins and over-sized Christmas gifts. These windows were made up of small squares of glass, squeezed together; the products and scenes displayed were tiny and detailed as if Swiss precision had crossed the mountains. The shops gave off a warm intimate light, from old-fashioned single bulbs in the ceiling, rather than fluorescence. I had seen towns like this, in the pages of children's storybooks. Every second shop seemed to be a tea room where well-dressed Europeans sipped cocoa, sucked on homemade confections rolled in icing sugar, letting chocolate melt in their mouths. These were the last days before Christmas. Far off in the cities, the streets and department stores would be madness; here, there was a rare stillness and beauty under clear dark skies. Wandering around the streets with their promise of Christmas, I felt distant from the others, knowing that when we returned to Spain, they were going home to the harried pleasure of family Christmases—they were full of those false complaints about the season's chores. I'd be staying in my downtown Barcelona apartment, trying to cobble together a Christmas the way expatriates do.

But loneliness evaporates as we climb the steps of the ancient stone church where we are to perform Haydn's oratorio *The Creation*. Here we are: a Catalan choir, an English orchestra, an Austrian composer, a German text based on a Hebrew Bible scripture and an English epic poem (Milton's *Paradise Lost*), an Italian and Swiss audience, and, further to the theory that you cannot go anywhere in the world and not find a Newfoundlander, I am in the mix.

There's anticipatory silence in the sparse church. Our concert dress is flimsy and feels colder still looking out at the audience, wisely settled in their outerwear, their colourful scarves and hats distracting for the moment as we stand patiently during the business of tuning. The oboist—sure but discreet—strikes a tuning fork against his knee, puts it tight to his ear and listens; with the A 440 clear in his head, he sounds the pitch that will tune the orchestra. The strings muck around, so much last minute tinkering; the winds make shorter work of it. Then everything fades, and the audience's bright clothing slips into our peripheral vision, disappearing altogether as we focus.

The orchestra begins eerily, cautiously, as if creeping along an unknown passage. Occasional ominous chords hint at the drama to come, but it is drama reined in, a prolonged, contained drama. In the midst of this representation of chaos, the angel Raphael eases himself in and prepares the listeners quietly, briefly, for the news the choir will bring—the announcement that the Lord has said, "Let there be ... LIGHT." And in that moment, a grand fortissimo erupts from the choir and the orchestra and the burst of joy inside each and every singer is palpable, as if you are walking at night and with no preparation or explanation, suddenly you are flooded in light. The switch has been activated. God has ended the creation process. The tenor, Uriel, announces cheerily that gloom and chaos are ended; the choir describes hell's spirits forced back into the abyss—they go in despairing, cursing rage, into eternal night. Then, a tender, lyrical celebration of this news: there is a *new* world. *Und eine neue Welt entspringt auf Gottes Wort*—we sing, *A new world springs forth at God's word.*

We stand and listen as the angel, Uriel, relates the story with lines of Biblical text and hints and influences from *Paradise Lost*; when we are not singing, we fall into wonderment as we listen. But we have a role to play; our continuity and commentary are sprinkled through the work. When Adam and Eve sing the world's first duet, pizzicato (plucked) strings tiptoe in triplets as the pair sings—tentatively, gingerly, as if marvelling at their very existence. The choir tenderly punctuates what is happening, as if trying not to intrude on the new pair. Adam and Eve surely cannot hear the mantra of praise gently intoned by the choir— *Blessed be His power, His name be ever magnified*—as this is outside their private moment. We focus—listening, blending, remembering phrasing and dynamics. We're working our bodies—lips, face muscles, and diaphragms. No athlete on the field or in the weight room is working any harder. We are rooted to the task at hand, executing the nuances we have rehearsed and new ones demanded now by the conductor. Yet, at the same time, we have left this worldly chorister's arena of being too hot or too cold, of sore legs and tired arms, of trying not to sneeze, of suppressing a cough—we have left all that behind and wandered onto a higher plane.

In early summer we travelled again, this time to Montpellier to perform at Festival Radio France. We sang a concert version of Verdi's opera *Joan of Arc*. We stood there in our stifling outfits: black tuxedos for men, long-sleeved white blouses and black skirts for women. It was hot, midday or early afternoon. We were not far from the Riviera where bathers romped in the waves and lolled in the sun, but we were standing on our risers in an outdoor makeshift theatre in the full power of the scorching sun.

Here we are: I think I am going to die from the heat; the others can hardly bear it and they are Mediterranean. *La chica de Terra Nova* (I was often referred to in the choir as "the girl from Newfoundland") is wilting, expiring. The baton drops and Verdi the dramatist is off. It is hard to believe this man had not experienced Hollywood. What kind of film scores he would have given us had he worked there. The drama is terrifying and yet, in Verdi fashion, minutes later the musical landscape has changed. From the opening—with its fast, furious strings hammering at us, scaring us, telling us that something terrifying is going to happen—to suddenly, over pizzicato strings, a lone flute singing a simple plaintive phrase. The clarinet follows, then the oboe. We hear a polite dialogue—each one handing off a line to the others—that eases into a tender woodwind trio. This should be enough to bring any listener immediately into the opera, but if not, wait: the great chorus will soon enter. We watch the conductor, we listen to the orchestra, we are ready. One of our first words is a forceful "*Maladetti!*" ("Curse you!"). And then I am lost, lost in the score, in the rush of sound in the drama of the Maid of Orleans—her story, the unfairness of it all, the heroism, the horror, the defiance, the bravery, her faith. I am part of it! Me, *La Mahjahree*, almost expired from the blazing sun. I am there, part of this huge swelling Mediterranean chorus, this gusty gutsy sound. Oh Glory! I am Italian, Catalan, Spanish, I am Verdi's neighbour, I am a French peasant, I'm a personal friend of Joan of Arc—I'm just plain horrified at the tragedy that's about to unfold. I fear, I shake, quake, tremble, I pray, believe, trust, feel, hope—then sink into despair.

That is how it is with choral singing. The audience sees composure, discipline, training—a uniform, impeccably groomed group. But they don't see what's inside—a collection of individual packages of love and loss, joy and pain, memory and desire—the contents spilling out through the most emotive instrument of all, the voice.

Two hours later, exhausted, parched, nearly dead from heat prostration, I will walk on air, on water, so great is the glory of what we've done. My fellow choristers will trip over themselves to find a snack truck that sells Perrier. I will search in vain for an orange Popsicle.

Reels, Rock and Rosaries: Confessions of a
Newfoundland Musician, 2005

My Twin Passions:
Music and Newfoundland

I REMEMBER my first book.

The cover is light green, uncluttered; the title and scant information, mysterious to me at the time, appears in a darker green. In the centre of this pale sea floats a small, stark image—a silhouette of the island of Newfoundland; floats but surely is anchored because it is fixed and solid.

The island's configuration is rich, intricately designed as if the geo-gods of rock and glacier made merry mapping us out— grinding out inlets and coves by the thousands around 6,000 miles of rocky coastline. Is that how we came to be? Or did celestial artisans work the land like putty, moulding and shaping, pushing and pulling? Or perhaps child-gods drawing on a sandy beach grabbed a shared stick from one another, saying: I want to shove this in, poke that out. However it happened, we've ended up on a distinctive rock. Who, having seen the map of the island of Newfoundland, cannot identify it again?

Perhaps that is why the small green book—not a myopic view of my thumb, not the bottle (I mean the baby bottle)—is my primal image, the first one I remember, the one that has endured. That wannabe triangle with its long deep bays and small jagged coves sent its curious peninsulas out to me. They crawled into my muscles, bones, and sinews carrying a message: Newfoundland was an island country, and we a people.

The facts belie this. By the time I was born, Newfoundland had become a province of Canada, but I cannot say for sure when that news reached me—maybe a couple of years ago at a cocktail party? But that we were a nation apart, that there was an "us" wrapped up in that tiny figure was clear to me. The cover told a story: the vastness and expanse of the implied water declared a gulf between us and others. And, as in the tongue-in-cheek maps of the world sold here as souvenirs, the location of the island proclaimed Newfoundland as the centre of the world.

Was this, the cover design of my father's 1955 *Old-Time Songs of Newfoundland*, his ultimate act of patriotism?

The silhouette, a lone raft in a clear sea, sat temptingly on the cover, as alluring as a desktop icon. I double-clicked at an early age, and walked in. Walked into pages of sailors and loggers, sealers and lovers, roaming the waters and beaches of some certain country. I couldn't read, but others could, and when they gathered around the piano at home to sing, I held up my book, turned pages, and jumped in when I could grab onto a familiar word or line. It was like skipping Double Dutch with bigger kids—the grown-ups were efficient, faster, and I could only hope to dodge in when something familiar whizzed by. I rhymed off the names of "Jim Fling, Tom Ring and Johnson, champion of the ring" piling into a soiree at Kelligrews, a party already jam-packed with "Jim Brine, Din Ryan, Flipper Smith and Caroline." I sang about the O'Hooligans hosting a tea party with a cake so tough that "two sealers attacked it with hand-spikes to try to remove the top crust." There was Jim Long boasting about how to get the girl you want, the braggart Jack Hinks, rebels, pranksters, and sooks whining about unrequited love.

Balladeers, some long gone, most with their identities forgotten, had eavesdropped, spied, recorded incidents they'd witnessed and stories they'd heard. Sometimes faithful photographers, sometimes imaginative painters, they left us with the details and drama of lives lived on and around a cold sea. I didn't always understand the lyrics of our songwriters who, far from the shores of the American dream, recorded also that hard work leads to more hard work, and often to a cycle of futility and bitterness.

> *Two dollars they'll pay you for piling up timber,*
> *And then eighteen dollars for board they will take,*
> *And then they will take six dollars for blankets;*
> *And that's how you're soaked on the shores of Twin Lakes.*
>   ("Twin Lakes")

It was bustling in those pages: competitive whalers racing across the Atlantic; men (real men, names listed) fighting storms at sea, sometimes winning, often not. Stories of seals caught, lives lost, a litany of shipwrecks, and tales of highjinks on the squid-jigging ground. The songs described not the beauty of the land but the power of the sea. It was an aural jumble to a small child, but breathless and vivid. After a night of singing the songs from my little green book, I fell into bed exhausted from travels around my vibrant island country.

This was my earliest music. Then, a few years later, I rose from a small oak desk in my Grade 1 classroom and took my first steps into that expansive country of classical music. The entryway was my first piano lesson.

It was momentous: the departure from the safe, known world of school across no man's land to the adjoining convent, tentatively creeping along the wide dark corridor lit only by a red vigil lamp, arriving at last into a bright open palatial room, Mother Patricia's parlour. The aged nun, the height of the ornate ceilings, the grandeur of the windows flashed that this was a life-changing moment. In the coming weeks, as the curious blotches on the page unscrambled and connected with the black and white piano keys, the miracle of reading music was mine. How was I so lucky—why me, to have this grand introduction, to decipher a foreign language that would ease me into a lifetime of riches and plenty, the gift given early, the gift no child should be deprived of. And where that led! To glee club, where I swear I levitated when I first heard four-part harmony, where I myself was in the bundle of notes creating that marvel of sound, in the crush, the warm squeeze, the dissonance waiting to resolve. The simple skill of musical literacy led to friendships, to travel, to a passport that permitted entry to musical ensembles anywhere. Led to a place where street language doesn't matter, where a greater shared language transcends all. Led to a key to a private club that has branches all over the world.

Then orchestral music gathered me up and lured me into a sea of chords and colours, of harmonies parading by, of melodies chasing one another. It offered the wild ride through Leonard Bernstein's overture to *Candide*; I, the piccolo player, surfing above the orchestra then falling, falling into a hole dug by panic and terror, the hole where the solo's supposed to be. And next night getting a second crack at it, certain I'll make it this time, and yes I arrive, right at the spot where the solo comes, no hole this time—just a small crash landing on the wrong note.

Classical music stood fast, but Newfoundland music swirled around me, too. In the 1970s a groundswell of nationalism pushed traditional music forward, energizing and re-creating it, and I embraced all that—getting a phone call from an excited friend with hot news: The Duff (Figgy Duff) would be playing here, or singing there—saying yes, yes to all of it, and all of it gloriously tied to a new heightened expression of patriotism, revelling in the swelling numbers of those who felt the passion, grabbed music as a vehicle, grasped it as a symbol.

This was in my early working years; I tagged along with the crowd, taking on the habits of reporters from the old days, coursing late night watering holes. Released from our Duckworth Street newsroom, we would escape into the circuit of The Cochrane, The Welcome, Freddy's (The Royalton), Bridgett's, The Belmont, Dirty Dick's—ending up in after-hours hideaways at 4 a.m., worn out from dancing jigs and reels with fallen and falling colleagues. Our heels and toes cast about in those fly-away gestures—joy, pride, and anger all kicked up in those flying steps. Never-ending energy pushing never-ending music. You couldn't stop, even though your sore, aching hips begged you to. If you dropped down dead, they'd dance around you, because who could rein in the pulsing rhythm, who could abandon the dance?

I could. One foot was lodged there in the traditional music revival but, no matter how grand it was, no matter how true, my other foot itched to head home to lose myself in recordings of Elly Ameling singing Schubert or Georg Solti conducting Brahms. I listened to traditional music with one ear, just waiting to trot off next night to orchestra practice, flute tucked protectively under my arm, squirming a little knowing that for some, in those days, the house of Newfoundland nationalism held no room for classical music.

The flute, too, got tangled up in the opposing impulses of my musical life. I canvassed the town until I found a jeweller brave enough and skilled enough to drill a hole into my precious silver Haines flute. He soldered on a tiny metal plate so I could snap on a microphone. On Tuesdays and Sundays I would attend orchestra rehearsals for a Haydn symphony or a Tchaikovsky piano concerto; the rest of the week I pretended I was Jethro Tull or Herbie Mann. The waves of rock music tossed me into a hazy new world of enhanced listening, lost in the roar of the Rolling Stones and Pink Floyd. Rock hung around—I grabbed it, rolled in it when I needed to convince myself I'd travelled beyond the long arm of the convent school. But when I sought ecstasy, exhilaration, or catharsis, I hauled out recordings of Schumann and Brahms and let their great symphonies wash over me. I was always in the closet, bumping around contradictions, even today in aerobics class where I can bounce and flop and bop to music I am officially in rebellion against. (I disguise myself to maintain a healthy public disassociation from pop, disco, and other low-lying musical disorders.) Country music came late. No coincidence that just as I needed the hurtin' songs, the hurtin' songs arrived—I simply hadn't "heard" them before. When Patsy Cline strutted in with her raw, earthy sensibility, the pining heroes of Franz Schubert were shoved out—but only temporarily.

Music kept circling me. Wherever I moved, music was there too. I fell into broadcasting and after commentary, journalism, and satire, I settled comfortably into hosting a late-night classical music program. The intimacy of radio and the vulnerability that steals in at night brought stacks of letters from restless insomniacs, solitary night-shift workers and vigil-keepers watching over the ill and the dying. Truck drivers on their long-distance runs kept company with the show, as did young lovers like Lindsay M. in Edmonton and Mark S. in Regina. They were in a long-distance relationship. They lay in separate beds, in distant cities, linked by music they were listening to "together."

The power of music was not news to me. Not since sitting in a box in an opera house, Gran Teatre del Liceu in Barcelona, close enough to sweat and tremble with Agnes Baltsa and José Carreras as they lured us into the passion and horror of Georges Bizet's *Carmen*. No, the power of music was not new to me—not since I'd had to forsake choral music in the early years of my apostasy, because the childhood knot of music and religion was too tight to undo. The daily mail to the radio show brought not news but a reminder that notes and chords are loaded with pleasure and pain, that for many the trigger for memory, more than taste or smell or even photographs, is aural. A reminder that the stream that flows between now and then, between present and past, is music.

In Newfoundland music, the themes have changed since the songs of my childhood. Many songwriters now are the voice of the migrant worker; themes are often home, emigration, yearning and longing. Those away are nostalgic for home, those here nostalgic for the past. Around the letters, profiles, memories, and photos in the glossy magazine *The Downhomer*, the Newfoundland saga unfolds in the pages of advertisements for moving companies and real estate. In all the shifting and resettling, the coming and going, music stands as connector.

A few years ago my 88-year-old aunt travelled from Arizona to St. John's to attend her sister's (my mother's) birthday. She'd left Newfoundland in the 1940s and had been back maybe two or three times. There was music in our houses each evening she was here—either us playing and singing around the piano or recordings in the background. On one of those nights, she was relating to me a story about the distant past when suddenly she stopped speaking, drifted off. She was listening. The Walsh family CD *The Passing of the Years* was playing. My aunt turned to me and said, "The only time I hear music is when I'm home." *Home.* She'd been gone 60 years. It's not possible that she hadn't heard music in a lifetime of raising children and grandchildren, but what she'd heard passed her by until that moment, when a clear, sweet voice sang a sentimental song that wound its way deep into the soul of this Newfoundland emigré.

The shape of the island of Newfoundland has been forged into brooches and pendants, and it hangs as earrings off the heads of young and old. It's imprinted on jackets, T-shirts, scarves, and lingerie. (And yes, there are tattoos.) Are we peculiar? Are the inhabitants of Alberta and Ontario roaming the world with little Canadas dangling off their necks? That first image of mine, that small odd triangle poked and prodded with permutations and indentations, is for me more than a geological formation. It is a symbol of place, home, nationhood. Against these backdrops of Newfoundland and music, my life has fallen.

Reels, Rock and Rosaries: Confessions of a
Newfoundland Musician, 2005

Regarding *Regarding Our Father*

MY WRITING life began with short declarative sentences. (*Christmas is coming.*) Phrases expanded as vocabulary grew. I basked in language and at the same time learned to be choosy. Writing for radio and columns tightened my prose until one day I broke free of the straightjacket of those genres and lolled around in longer forms: I allowed myself to "inhabit the essay." Expanding, contracting, accruing words, eschewing words— that was the seesaw, the ebb and flow of my writing life. Then I encountered the world of film, the word script. Here I am stingy. I jingle my small pouch of words. I must spend wisely.

From radio I'd learned the lessons of an aural medium— readers can't linger; they hear the words once—and precision. Like most writers, I carry a pencil to the podium even if I'm reading from a published piece. Always at the last minute a change must be made, you find the better word. Sitting in a studio laying down film narration after the picture lock is done, no second chance exists. You can alter a phrase, but what you say and how you say it must match exactly the timing of what you replace. No accommodation for a syllable more, or less.

My brother John Doyle and I have co-written/directed a 45-minute documentary about our father, Gerald S. Doyle. *Regarding Our Father* tells the story of this businessman and folksong collector using the 16 mm colour footage he shot as he travelled outport Newfoundland and coastal Labrador in the 1930s, 1940s, and 1950s.

Here is the trajectory of the project: A man stands on the deck of his boat as it motors into a small community in, say, 1939. The keen observer captures as much as he can on tiny three-minute reels of celluloid. Seascapes, landscapes, sunsets (our father *loved* a Bonavista Bay sunset), and people. Men, women, and children, standing, laughing, working, fishing, making fish, rowing in dories, playing in punts, piling into trap skiffs to attend Mass in a neighbouring community. Nuns (live ones) in a cemetery. Shopkeepers with customers. Passengers in coastal boats on the move.

The rolls of film were secured with elastic, returned to their packages, and sent off for processing. Back would come the familiar 4-inch yellow boxes. An occasional scrawl from Dad's fountain pen might hint at time or place. The pile of mostly unopened boxes grew until his death. Our mother sold the family home in 1963 and, over her many moves, the white tin portable cupboard now sagging with its unseen gems travelled with her until finally it was deposited in my brother's basement. John is the filmmaker in the family. Through the years those yellow boxes beckoned, nagged, burdened, and lured him until one day he faced into the task. He viewed every single shot, every frame, 70 years after the camera's eye first opened. He knew a film must be made and in time signed on a recalcitrant sibling, for whom the word *fillum* still means the small black coil you load into your Brownie.

The writer's nemesis, the blank screen, is not found here; in its place are thousands of pictures, thousands of frames recorded by a patriot watching his country and its people. Images flick by on the screen, images captured long ago but new to us. We stare at them open-mouthed, astonished as the country of Newfoundland unfolds on the small viewer of the AVID, the monstrous editing table at Newfoundland Independent Filmmakers Co-Operative (NIFCO). I sneak a sideways look at my brother, creeping toward the age of the man on the screen. The father and son will connect here at an exact age. We have spent a long time on this adventure.

Private journeys take us back to childhood, to photographer John's darkroom and a young pest demanding to be allowed in and moments later clamouring to be let out. Not a slit of light could be admitted, not enough for a kid sister to squeeze through. Being closeted in the squatty dark editing suite didn't feel much different—at first. Then Dad walked.

He is walking up the back driveway of our house, walking toward the camera. I had never seen him walk. Later the camera flicks on me and I smile at the cameraman. I now own scenes, moments where I can say, *yes*. We did dwell in the same universe. We did play on the same lawn, stand on the deck of the same boat, and feel the same salt air and brisk winds blow over us.

I was a small child when my father died, too young to grieve— then. Old enough, though 40 years later slogging home from NIFCO in bleak February days after watching my father come alive on the screen. We grew up looking at a corporate photo of him, probably taken near the time illness overtook him. He was always old, or so it seemed. (He died at 63.) Now his personality is released as we see him gesture, laugh, sing with friends.

I will remain forever grateful to my father for his forethought to shoot the film, to my mother for preserving it, and to my brother who laboured (hard labour) to bring the buried treasure to the surface. And to those who on occasion snatched the camera and stole up on Dad until he caught on. Every single shot of him ends with the same dismissive gesture, the wave to turn off the camera. John points out: At $13.25 a roll, small wonder.

The blank page won't daunt me again. I see it now as freedom. A script is restrictive in a documentary like ours driven by the footage. Pictures tell the story here; the subservient words must fall in line with the images. The script—those handfuls of words used to support or to link—becomes the slave, not the master. That transfer of power can leave the print writer bereft.

Our father lived to see the realization of his ideas. He founded a firm that prospered; he collected, published, and distributed folksongs; he created a nightly radio broadcast with news and a unique message service. He sired seven sons and a daughter. What was his ambition for the films? Surely not a movie made by two of his children 80 years after his camera first whirred. In an age when a video is shot and posted minutes later, there is something sweet and precious about this long slow manifestation.

The marvel of it. We engaged in an artistic enterprise with our long dead father. For Dad is the filmmaker, the first member of the crew. *Regarding Our Father* begins with him.

WORD, Winter, 2012

Coming to a Farm Near You?

GEORGE BUSH shoots quail with a shotgun—a weapon powerful enough to send an accidental human target to hospital. I replay the scene in my mind: Bush and pals on the ranch firing shot, tiny birds dropping from the sky. I squint, trying desperately to see Pamela Anderson or Paul McCartney hovering there, speechifying about innocent animal victims. No sign.

Of course they're not there. If they showed up, the result wouldn't be high-minded rhetoric and a photo-op. It would probably be a glimpse of them wrapped, not in bright red snowsuits, but prison garb. Not so pretty.

You don't see them, either, prowling around Alberta farm country or hassling blue-collar workers as they head into cold jobs in slaughterhouses and packaging plants. You don't see them because they wouldn't last. I'm not saying Albertans are rough. I'm saying they speak with a clear voice. And Ralph Klein is blessed with the ability to be unequivocal.

But if international activists are sincere in wanting to stop the killing of animals, why aren't they aiming at significant targets? They have multi-million dollar public relations machinery. They have endless time, too—not because they are devoted volunteers, but because they are highly paid corporate employees. And they have an inestimable advantage: the energy of the self-righteous.

Religion has taught us the power—and danger—of that ingredient. With such a powerhouse in place, why are they hanging around a few ice pans in a tiny corner of eastern Canada? Why beat down a working-class pursuit on a remote island, while MacDonald's and Burger King order up newly killed animals for millions of North Americans, daily?

It makes no sense. It would be like creating an army to wipe out pornography and instead of mobilizing against the industry, you station troops on a sidewalk in Mississauga and relentlessly stalk two guys who rent soft porn on Friday nights.

The Newfoundland sealer has been targeted and demonized in the international protest against the killing of animals. Sir Paul and Lady (I use the word loosely) McCartney donned their glamorous armour and went to the ice. They saw no seals killed, saw no sealers. There was no hunt. That didn't stop the American TV show *Larry King Live* from tacitly suggesting the McCartneys were witnessing baby seals being clubbed. The station ran edited, outdated footage from a special interest group throughout the one-hour interview. A few words identified the footage, but a small running line is as good as invisible when the screen is filled with sensational images. The McCartneys see themselves as heroes. I'll nominate them for a bravery award after they invade Bush territory and nag him about unsuspecting quail.

Speaking of America, where is it in this campaign? There's a seal hunt in Alaska. There's one in Quebec, too. But, was it Moses or Trudeau who commanded: Thou shalt not criticize Quebec? I don't want to see more sealers tormented, but if "Quebec" preceded "sealer" every time the word appears in the media, activists would be banished from Canada.

Paul McCartney loomed large from that giant TV screen and, with the same certainty with which he and his wife delivered "facts," reported he was in Newfoundland. He was in PEI. Most of us would find it hard to forge on after such an error, but carry on they did. I wanted to weep for their public humiliation—but the tears just wouldn't flow.

Pamela Anderson used (abused) her hosting gig at the Junos to get a berth in Paul McCartney's popular wagon. It's crowded there now with has-beens, wannabes, and assorted attention-getters. She didn't look like those hardy protestors— she wasn't bundled in as many layers—but she surfed on the same smugness.

Like all the activists who swear allegiance to defenceless animals, she forgot to mention hard-hearted Maine fishermen who trick lobsters into fatal traps. She forgot sports fishermen in Minnesota who idle away weekends casting colourful flies to lure trout onto deadly hooks. Cattle and sheep farmers, chuckling Colonel Sanders, and cheerful George W. out for a shoot—they've all managed to escape the wrath of the activists. *So far.*

Imagine a remote highway in Alberta. One morning just outside a farm, as close as they can go without trespassing, a band of zealots from the United States or England swarm the property. They provoke the farmers. They move from there to packaging plants and slaughterhouses, taunting men and women as they go to work. How long would this be tolerated?

Heather McCartney, on *Larry King Live*, repeated scripted lines like a—like a trained seal. She was scary. But is she ever scared?

I have the idea that if animal activists turned up on prairie farms, they wouldn't be giving press conferences and posing for photo-ops.

Help, Albertans! Tell us what to do.

Calgary Herald, April 9, 2006

The Anti-Sealing Psalter

I'M SITTING in the second-storey window of an old house in rural Newfoundland. I'm looking out on Newfoundlandness, if I may coin a word. Ahead of me for miles is a grey rough sea and whitecaps. The wind is blowing so hard I fear for the lilac I planted last month. I put brin (you might call it burlap) around it, but perhaps concrete slabs would have been a more appropriate protector. To one side I can see the garden I tried to develop here on solid rock. Even after loads of kelp, peat moss, topsoil, and capelin, it still looks as if I took a jackhammer to a patch of sidewalk on Water Street and tried to plant chard there.

On my left, there's a cluster of houses around a horseshoe of water. And here we have it, that national irritant, that incendiary piece of turf, that little piece of humanity known as a Newfoundland outport. Looks innocuous enough, peaceful even—it's just a place where people live. But it's immortalized now as the breeding ground of that great barbarian, the Newfoundland sealer. My own grandfather, who was from this community, went to the ice 63 times, but he died long before he would have to hear himself described the world over in IFAW terms. I'm glad for him.

But the IFAW won't be hearing from me. I'll tell you quite frankly the effect they have on me: They enrage me, then the rage dissipates into defeat. I can think of no way to deal with them. To engage in statistical warfare is about as productive as name-calling. The argument, made for the thousandth time, that killing a seal is the same as killing a trout or any other animal, falls on deaf ears. And the fact that Newfoundlanders actually eat seal meat seems to be of no interest.

As for a public-relations campaign to counter theirs, I haven't got the bucks. If I had the face to set up an international organization designed to keep me and my friends employed, I'd have a machine in place. I could work full-time then, persuading people to believe in my cause, so that they could employ me to fight it. Nice work, if you can get it.

To tell you the truth, there's actually nothing about the IFAW that surprises me. Years ago, some people I know well fell into the hands of a fundamentalist from the American South. Before long, they stopped listening to radio and reading newspapers and magazines. They listened only to cassette tapes of their preacher laying out his interpretation of the Bible. They were not given to discussion because they "knew" they were right. They spent their time shoring up their membership and feeding each other with their sense of moral rectitude. Soon nothing mattered to them but the preservation of the cult. It's my familiarity with that fundamentalist fringe that enables me to understand the IFAW. It does nothing to make me accept them.

And now they have on board some of Canada's finest, including poets and singer-songwriters, who recently felt the need to bare their souls on the subject of seals. These good folk added their names to the hysterical advertisements that have been appearing under the banner of the IFAW. I expect any day to read of a press conference where Timothy Findley and Loreena McKennitt tell us how they feel about hamburgers and chops. Or are their sensibilities better able to hold up under the thought of slaughtered pigs and cows?

There's one thing I'm curious about with regard to the anti-sealing campaign. If the IFAW (with or without the poets) decided to go after the farmers of Alberta or Saskatchewan, how far would they get? Would provincial and federal governments stand by while the farms of the prairies became the workplace from hell? Would no agency or group in Canada raise a cry of protest against the harassment of workers and the destruction of an industry?

And if the IFAW decided to persecute the native people of Canada who hunt seals with the same zeal with which they hound Newfoundlanders, what would the response of Canadians be? There are many Canadians who would be reluctant to criticize the lifestyle, culture, or work of native people, but who don't feel the same delicacy about Newfoundlanders.

In the meantime, I was surprised on Saturday to see Timothy Findley novels and Loreena McKennitt CDs still for sale here. I would have thought they'd pull their products from this marketplace. Surely they are worried that money used to purchase their products might be blood money—you know, money made by sealers plying their trade.

But what do I know? This is an issue best described by the IFAW at their next synod.

Globe and Mail, December 15, 1997

Where Does the Culture Begin, and End?

I HAVE flat feet. I cope with this minor misery by wearing fibreglass inserts in my shoes. But that does nothing for the hours I spend in the woods, trouting.

One day I was having serious morning-after pains while I was chatting to a friend. I leaned down to massage my feet and muttered to myself: I must get lifts in my rubber boots. My friend laughed at the seeming incongruity between traditional Newfoundland footwear and "urbane" enhancements. That is so you, he said.

His remark could be a springboard for an essay on Newfoundland culture, covering what it is, what it isn't, how I'm sure I'm right, why I'm sure I'm wrong, and other explorations of self-doubt on the painful subject of "my people."

When I think of having to define Newfoundland culture, I draw a blank. I'm too hard on myself to allow sentimentality to creep into my ode to Newfoundland. So I go about it this way. I picture myself sitting in a tent in a desert in, say, Timbuktu. Someone who's never travelled asks me about Newfoundland. And I talk the big ball game, itemizing the things that make us us. Then I ruthlessly strike from the list typically Western phenomena, anything blatantly North American. I point to the now shrunken list and say, faintly: There you have it, that's it. Newfoundland culture.

But would there be anything left on the list?

In terms of my own lifestyle, traditions, habits, and hobbies, I've had to face hard facts. I've had my moments of truth and they've always taken place in the same spot: that 100-mile stretch of rough Atlantic, that Styx, between mainland Canada and the island of Newfoundland. I've come to look upon the ferry as a great soaking tank where fanciful notions are scrubbed off me. I disembark on this side dressed only in one hard fact: I've got more in common with those I've left behind than with those I'm coming back to.

The ferry can do that to you. You've been away a year or two, boasting about your native paradise. You know the island's history and politics. You can sing the songs and ballads. Your rhetoric alone will bring in thousands in tourist dollars. You are it: the quintessential Newfoundlander. You are … Miss Newfoundland.

Then you board the ferry.

"Salt of the earth," everyone around you is saying of the longshoremen directing traffic onto the boat. There's a lilt in their speech that brings a smile to your face; the old accents still linger. You swell with pride at the tourists' reaction to this "world next door." You rush to help visitors so they'll know you belong.

It's the cafeteria smell that brings the first moment of grief. Greasy fried food, chips drenched in batter, fish smothered with gravy. All you really want is a simple meal, a Greek salad maybe. Falafel. You walk out and head for the kiosk. Newfie souvenirs.

One day soon I will write a book that takes a hard look at Newfoundland "culture." I want to bring into this the history of my own consciousness as a Newfoundlander. This would cover my childhood, declared invalid by some because I didn't grow up in an outport and didn't have uncles who danced; my schooling, which was 19th-century Irish; and my university years, which drove home one thing: a sense that I was part of a colonized people, being recolonized every day. I would address, too, the 1970s, whence came the much-touted "Newfoundland Renaissance."

In my book, I will pick through the myths about New-foundland and look at the mythmakers. I want to examine the definitions of Newfoundland culture and the agenda of the definers. I want to write about the stultifying categorizations that abound in Newfoundland, the kind of thinking that is reflected in my friend's reaction to the harmless surgery I propose for my rubber boot!

Ah, the rubber boot. There's a novelist here who likes to insist he's not part of the "rubber boot culture." Is that remark comprehensible or contemptible? When academics from "away" began in the 1970s to wear rubber boots on perfectly dry days were they trying to show support for a traditional way of life in Newfoundland, or were they being just plain dumb? How absurd did they look to the outport kids sitting in their classrooms who'd rather swim to school than be made to walk there wearing rubber boots.

The millennium is just about spent. And reflecting on that is a noble thing. But I feel like spending some time thinking about my people.

Globe and Mail, June 28, 1999

On the Wings of Tobin's Rhetoric

THERE'S BEEN a rumour around for some months now that there will be a provincial election here this fall. Roads are being paved at an alarming rate. Even a lonely stretch of country road in my neighbourhood that has hardly a house on it is suddenly being resurfaced. Given the short term this administration has been in office (2½ years), and the absence of any justification for an election just now, it's hard not to see Brian Tobin looking opportunistic, in a familiar kind of way.

Premier Tobin has hinted he might need to go to the polls because talks have broken off with INCO over the Voisey's Bay nickel development. But there has not been enough public criticism of his stand, here in Newfoundland, to justify an election on this. The other political parties, as well as commentators and editorial writers, don't appear to be disagreeing with him in any significant way.

Whence, then, this impetus to hold an election? The timing is perfect. An already popular premier has lucked into, or perhaps even created, a *cause célèbre*. He can blaze into glory with pretty well the whole province on side, united against the corporate bully, symbol of all the bad deals Newfoundland has suffered through.

Mr. Tobin likes to grandstand. He is still savouring the sweet moments of his supposed triumph in the Turbot War of 1995, when he played Captain Tobin on the High Seas, commandeering the capture of a Spanish vessel. It's a role he played well. What I can't get over is the way everyone forgets—or perhaps some never knew—how much of that was bluster.

I've heard a thousand times about the *Estai* being brought into St. John's under arrest. One hardly ever hears another stage of that story: The *Estai* sailed out through the Narrows with turbot in the hold. I was in the hold of the *Estai* while it was in port, opened a box and saw the turbot. They were tiny, and the sight was disturbing. But it was no more disturbing than being in France later that year and seeing turbot everywhere on the menu. I cannot say I recognized any individual fish, but I did take away the definite impression that turbot were plentiful.

If there is an election, it will be fairly dull. I don't know what's happened in Newfoundland, but all of a sudden it seems everyone's a Liberal. Even old Tories seem to be Liberals. Consequently, the Conservatives have had trouble attracting a dynamic leader. The leader they do have is not likely to cause much of a stir in an election—or even in the House. And the NDP is a party of one; there is one lone New Democrat in the House of Assembly and the party seems to consist only of him.

There was a fourth fledgling party called the Newfoundland and Labrador Party, but a little while ago the interim leader disappeared. During her absence, press releases suggested all was well, they'd simply misplaced their leader. (It was reminiscent of the Newfoundland cult film *Faustus Bidgood*, in which the poet-premier goes missing but regularly sends clues to his whereabouts, in the form of rhyming quatrains.) The leader of the Newfoundland and Labrador Party did eventually resurface and, when asked where she'd been, said simply: "Nowhere, that I know of." (She spoke in prose.)

So, with that lineup, it doesn't seem likely an election here will be worth talking about. Meanwhile, Premier Tobin is sitting pretty. One sign of his confidence is his rhetoric. He's in full flight. He increasingly says things like, "What the people of Newfoundland and Labrador have to hear," and, "I want the people of Newfoundland and Labrador to reflect on this." Recently, listening to him talk at length on radio, I started to get up out of my pew—when I suddenly realized I wasn't in church.

Mr. Tobin is having that kind of effect on me, sounding more and more like a preacher with a patronizing "I know you know what's good for you" kind of approach. He has a small repertoire of mantras, and he's becoming downright hard to listen to.

In the absence of any serious opposition, and with the prospect now, if he chooses to call an election, of sailing into four more years of power, Mr. Tobin is starting to allow his rhetorical flights to go unchecked. He outdid himself recently in an interview when he said, referring to discussions with INCO over Voisey's Bay, "This kind of approach is not acceptable in 1998, and will not be acceptable any time in the next millennium."

It was heartening, in this era of fear and uncertainty, to hear the captain stay the main course.

Globe and Mail, August 24, 1998

Mount Cashel for Sale

FOR SALE: fine old establishment and acres of prime real estate in St. John's east. Must sell fast. Management wants out.

Indeed, the Congregation of Christian Brothers is probably counting the days to the closure of their 90-year-old Mount Cashel Orphanage. They must hope that when the doors close, it will be the beginning of the end of the greatest crisis they've ever faced.

But the Brothers' closing the institution is like an alcoholic throwing out the booze in his house. It gets rid of the immediate problem, but it's not a long-term solution. There are too many other venues of temptation.

Mount Cashel is an institution where serious and harmful wrongdoing to young boys allegedly took place. But Mount Cashel is only a building. The problem is centred upon what went on inside. The Brothers have chosen to close an institution, but maybe they are missing the larger point—is it the Congregation, perhaps, that needs closing down?

This is not an extreme statement. Nor is it something the Brothers themselves have control over. It may well be that the choice to carry on their apostolate is not theirs. The happenings here in Newfoundland must be widely known in other areas where the Brothers operate—Toronto, Vancouver, and the West Indies. Are the Brothers still wanted there?

Surely their tarnished image is causing some anxiety for parents, school boards, and the church in these areas. And their financial situation can't be great these days—with the legal fees and the lawsuits that they are facing.

Perhaps the Brothers are considering folding. Certainly, their decision to leave Mount Cashel is an admission of defeat. They are saying that they can no longer guarantee their work, so to speak. They can't control what goes on in their institutions. They can't promise that boys won't be tampered with.

For the alleged victims of the sexual crimes at Mount Cashel, the announcement of the closure may have brought some sense of satisfaction, of vengeance, or of being vindicated. And never in their wildest imaginings could they have foreseen the present turn of events.

They may have been powerless as institutionalized children— no one listening to them, no one acting on their behalf. But they are being listened to now, and the decision by the Brothers to close the orphanage is a symbol of this phenomenal reversal of power.

But as Mount Cashel closes, there are still unanswered questions. Some of these will be addressed by the Hughes Inquiry, some in court, and some in civil lawsuits. These examinations will concentrate on the 1970s.

But what of all the other years? Does Mount Cashel go down in history as an institution where things got out of hand during one administration, with the rest of its history and image preserved intact? This was the Mount Cashel whose garden party was the event of the season, the Mount Cashel that boasted an excellent band and that toured the island with productions of Gilbert and

Sullivan musicals. There were other charming aspects, like the arrival every year—from a mystery donor—of a gigantic edible Christmas cake. And of course there was the raffle.

But, if all was well during those years—the 1940s, 1950s, 1960s—where are the defenders? Bishop Alphonsus Penney said recently that "the vast majority of the brothers fulfilled their vocation with unimpeachable integrity." But how does he speak with such certainty? With what authority? There must be hundreds of men in this town who have vivid memories of what it was like in the orphanage. If it was good in the good old days, why isn't someone saying so? I mean someone who'd know from first-hand experience.

There were a lot of smiling faces at the celebration of the Christian Brothers' Centenary in Newfoundland. And they're preserved in a book called *The Brothers Are Coming*. But maybe no one cares to recall that year just now. It was 1975-76, and while church and state were paying tribute to the Brothers' 100-year contribution in Newfoundland, a few small boys had another perspective.

Too bad they weren't asked to speak at the opening dinner.

CBC Radio, November 1989

How Long Does It Take to Forget Nationhood?

IN THREE weeks, on March 31, Newfoundland—and I presume Canada—will celebrate the 50th anniversary of Newfoundland's entry into Confederation. We joined just before the stroke of midnight that day. The next morning the carillon of the Peace Tower in Ottawa rang out a song it had never rung before: the Newfoundland folksong *The Squid-Jiggin' Ground*, which begins, "Oh, this is the place where the fishermen gather …"

Yes, Newfoundland became a province of Canada on March 31, 1949, and many consider that to be cause for great rejoicing. But March 31, 1949, was also the day that the country of Newfoundland ceased to exist. And that, too, must surely be marked. I for one will not let it go unnoted.

There are formidable forces in our society that are trying to extinguish nationalistic feelings in Newfoundland and to discredit those who question Confederation. Well-mannered, sensible people are sitting at dinner parties pronouncing that anyone who has doubts about Confederation is crazy. John Crosbie was quoted in the national press using the word "obtuse" to describe those who wonder whether Confederation was the right choice.

I offer a few comments.

One: The people who remain unconvinced about Confederation are intelligent, informed people who are merely raising a reasonable question: What on balance has been the result for us? What is true—and not true—at the end of the day? These people want to challenge the accepted canon that we were a desperate people incapable of handling our own affairs, that we are grateful for the salvation and paternalism Canada has offered. Some say the price of Confederation was too high, echoing a fear expressed in an 1860s ballad: "For a few thousand dollars of Canadian gold, don't let it be said that your birthright was sold."

Two: When you hear of the disease and poverty of Newfoundland in the 1920s and 1930s, ask yourself about your own corner of Canada. We did not have a monopoly on misery. Albertans ate gophers; in the Maritimes, unemployment was rampant. If you're reading this piece in Cabbagetown in Toronto, read Hugh Garner's novel of that name.

Three: There is much talk in Newfoundland about conspiracy theories, a range of scenarios suggesting that England and Canada manipulated us. Ask yourself this: Is that so hard to believe? Is it inconceivable that a small, poor place was a pawn in a deal between two greater powers?

Four: How long does it take to forget nationhood? Just for a moment, imagine that Canada is subsumed by the United States. How many years would it take before you felt about July 4 as you now feel about July 1? How long before *The Star Spangled Banner* would stir you? And if you have children who are 15 or 20, how long before they would become true Americans? Would there be Canadian spillage into the households they set up? Feelings don't die because your passport changes. To quote a line from a Ron Hynes song: "Out here between wind and flame, between tears and elation, lies a secret nation."

Five: In human terms, consider what it was like in Newfoundland on the night of March 31, 1949. For some it was a political victory, sweet as those things are. But for the rest? Of those who voted yes, many did so reluctantly. I have had people tell me that they voted for Confederation because of the benefits they believed would come to the old people, but they did not vote happily or without regret. And what of those who voted no, who couldn't bear the thought of losing their country? Knowing the level of passion and patriotism, of deep connection to this place, I find it hard to think about that night. Tom Cahill's play *As Loved Our Fathers* offers insight into the pain and hurt among divided families.

Six: There are those who like to think that this event is remote. But that is to denigrate many people. Every Newfoundlander over 50—those living here and those in the great diaspora—was born a Newfoundlander. Those who are 65 were teenagers at the time of Confederation. Those who are 70 and older voted.

In the midst of the coming hoopla, pause a moment to think of the Newfoundland people that night: the poor patriots, the privileged patriots, those who'd voted yes and those who'd voted no, those on both sides who were full of lingering uncertainties. Think of them going to bed that night Newfoundlanders and waking the next morning in a new country.

As for me on March 31, I take my cue from Ebenezer Scrooge who, speaking of another occasion, said: You keep it in your own way, and let me keep it in mine.

Globe and Mail, March 10, 1999

About the Author

MARJORIE DOYLE is a former columnist with the *Globe and Mail* and the *Evening Telegram*. Her work has appeared in many journals and newspapers including *Descant, Geist, Queen's Quarterly, The Fiddlehead, The Antigonish Review, Newfoundland Quarterly, National Post,* and *Calgary Herald.*

As a broadcaster, Doyle hosted the national CBC Radio program *That Time of the Night,* and was heard frequently on *Gabereau, Morningside, Stereo Morning,* and *The Arts Tonight.* She also appeared on *Pamela Wallin and Company, The Journal,* and *Canada AM.*

Her awards include Silver in the National Magazine Awards, two CBC Radio Awards for Programming Excellence, and a nomination for a Golden Sheaf Award. She participated in the Banff Writing Studio and has read across Canada, including at the Royal Ontario Museum. In 2009 she was Writer-in-Residence at Haig-Brown House on Vancouver Island.

Doyle holds an MA from Memorial University of Newfoundland, where she has taught creative non-fiction.

Doyle has lived in Switzerland, Spain, Wisconsin, Illinois, Toronto, and Calgary. She now lives in her native St. John's.